Preaching Through the Bible

1 Samuel

Michael Eaton

Sovereign World

Sovereign World
PO Box 777
Tonbridge
Kent TN11 9XT
England

By the same author:

Ecclesiastes (Tyndale Commentary) – IVP
The Baptism with the Spirit – IVP
How to Live a Godly Life – Sovereign World
How to Enjoy God's Worldwide Church – Sovereign World
Walk in the Spirit – Word
Living Under Grace (Romans 6–7) – Nelson Word

ISBN: 1 85240 172 9

Typeset by CRB Associates, Norwich
Printed in England by Clays Ltd, St Ives plc

Preface

There is need of a series of biblical expositions which are especially appropriate for English speaking preachers in the Third world. Such expositions need to be laid out in such a way that they will be useful to those who put their material to others in clear points. They need to avoid difficult vocabulary and advanced grammatical structures. They need to avoid European or North American illustrations. *Preaching Through the Bible* seeks to meet such a need. Although intended for an international audience I have no doubt that their simplicity will be of interest to many first-language speakers of English as well.

These expositions will take into account the Hebrew and Greek texts but will also take into account three translations of the Bible, the New King James (or Revised Authorized) Version, the New American Standard Version and the New International Version. The expositions will be comprehensible whichever of these three versions is used, and no doubt with some others as well. At times the expositor will simply translate the Hebrew or Greek himself.

It is not our purpose to deal with minute exegetical detail, although the commentator often has to do work of this nature as part of his preliminary preparation. But just as a good housewife likes to serve a good meal rather than display her pots and pans, so the good expositor is concerned with the 'good meal' of Scripture, rather than the 'pots and pans' of

3

dictionaries, disputed interpretations and the like. Only occasionally will such matters have to be discussed. Similarly matters of 'Introduction' do not receive detailed discussion. A simple outline of some 'introductory' matters is to be found in the appendix to the exposition but the first chapter gets immediately into the message of Scripture.

Michael A. Eaton

Contents

Contents

Author's Preface

This book of mine was written largely in South Africa. Earlier drafts were preached at Rouxville Baptist Church, Johannesburg (chapters 1–17), and were repeated at the Discipleship School of Chrisco Fellowship or at Chrisco's lunchtime meetings in Nairobi. The Evangelism and Reconciliation Ministries who held a mission at Gatundu, outside Nairobi, in Christmas 1993, also heard the early chapters. Some chapters first appeared in the magazines of Chrisco's Central Church and City Church.

Then the whole was rewritten while I was travelling round South Africa at the time of its first-ever multiracial election in May 1994. I had the privilege of preaching chapter 8 ('Rebuilding a Nation') during the earliest days of the new nation. 'God's Training' (of David) was preached also to ministers living in rural Gujarat in India. It was a joy to preach in the open-air in a valley between two hills, describing David and Goliath who also met in the open-air in a valley between two hills (1 Samuel 17:1–3).

I am grateful to my wife and family for their encouragement. Mrs Tina Gysling, my daughter, edited the last-but-one version of this work. My son Calvin has been an ever-present help in time of computer trouble. Also to Chris Mungeam for his enthusiasm and to Mrs Florence Okumu who has made many contributions to these pages – many thanks.

9

I specially pray these short expositions will be of use to my fellow preachers in my much-loved Kenya as well as in other parts of the world. May they help us to be faithful in the exposition of God's Word.

Michael A. Eaton

Chapter 1

One Individual Used By God
(1 Samuel 1:1–2:10)

The story of 1 and 2 Samuel begins by showing us how the personal problems of one individual can be something greatly used by God in the progress of his kingdom. Hannah was just one woman. One might ask what significance does one unknown woman have in the kingdom of God? Sometimes one person has a great part to play in what God is doing. That person may not be very famous or very important. He or she may be in the middle of some awful problem.

1. **God has a habit of using our personal problems**. Consider the first eight verses of 1 Samuel chapter 1. In some respects you would think Hannah might be quite happy. Her husband Elkanah came from a notable Levite family (see 1 Chronicles 6:16–26). His great-great-grandfather Zuph had the *'district of Zuph'* named after him (1 Samuel 9:5). Elkanah himself was gentle, considerate, a regular worshipper at Israel's centre of worship, Shiloh. As his polygamy reveals, he was a man of wealth.

But Hannah was unable to have children and lived in a culture that set a high value upon the number of children a man's wife had. Elkanah had turned to polygamy, a lapse from God's original intention but common – for those who could afford it – in Elkanah's day. A second wife had been taken in the hope of a child.

Polygamy either leads to strife or it involves the abandonment of close family life for the husband. In this case,

Peninah, the second wife was exceptionally unpleasant. Her provocation was deliberate and persistent. Hannah could not take the strain. Her husband did not understand. God did not seem to be in a hurry to answer prayer.

But as we are about to discover, God greatly used this problem of hers. It is through tribulations that we come into a rich experience of the kingdom of God. In the world we shall have tribulations, but God will use them and – if we allow him to do so – will carry forward his kingdom through our very troubles.

2. **What Hannah's troubles did for her was to drive her to pray** (1 Samuel 1:9–20). It is often easier for the people of God to pray when we are in bad trouble. It produces a kind of desperation in us. We give God more time. We are willing to come to terms with him. Trouble may lead us to pray with fervency, with energy, with determination, with persistency. Hannah was praying so fervently that Eli thought she was drunk. We ought to pray like this all the time, but when trouble comes along it often gives our praying a push in the right direction.

3. **Her troubles gave her the opportunity to forgive**. She had to forgive her husband for his tactlessness. She had to forgive Peninah for her perverse animosity. She had to forgive Eli for his false accusation. And she had to break through the feeling of being betrayed by God for his delayed help.

4. **A breakthrough came in her life when her will and God's will came together**. There came a point where she was ready to make a 'bargain' with God (1 Samuel 1:11). *'God, give me a son, and I'll give him to you to be brought up as a full-time worker in your temple,'* she prayed. God took her seriously. Actually that was precisely what he wanted. He needed a little boy as well! Because the leadership of Israel was so corrupt, what was needed was a young boy that God could reveal himself to and so start a new leadership in Israel altogether. When our will and God's will come together, things are likely to happen. The Holy Spirit was at work in leading Hannah to make this offer to God.

5. **Hannah's prayer was answered** (1 Samuel 1:19–28). But notice that she found peace before the answer came (1:18)! She was given the peace that passes all understanding simply by casting her care upon God, even though the answer had not yet come.

6. When the breakthrough came **it led Hannah into deeper and richer praise of God** (1 Samuel 2:1–10). Her psalm in 1 Samuel could have been a psalm that was already in existence. Or she may have written it herself. It certainly looks out to wider matters than her own concerns. She seems to have praised and worshipped God as energetically as she had put her requests to God before.

She glories in God's character, his holiness (2:2a), his uniqueness (2:2b), his reliability (2:2c), his knowledge (2:3c), his justice (2:3d).

She applies everything she knows about God to herself. She finds joy in him (2:1b), strength in him (2:1c). She finds courage not to be intimidated, as perhaps she had been by Peninah. *'My mouth boasts over my enemies'* (2:1b). She is expecting similar deliverances in the future.

She has come to see, through her experience of God's ways, that God rules the world. He rules over warriors and armies (2:4), over barren women (2:5), over life and death (2:6), over money (2:7–8). The very foundations of the world belong to the LORD (2:8b). If God can bring justice in a dispute between her and Peninah, she knows that God can do the same thing at a world-wide level. *'Those who oppose the LORD will be shattered'* (2:10).

She applies everything she has learnt not only to herself but to her nation. She is expecting God to send a king to Israel, and knows that he too will be protected in the same way she has been helped and protected.

So there are advantages in trials and tribulations. From them we learn God's ways and discover his greatness. In the end our knowledge of God is deepened. Amazingly, our troubles have a part to play in getting the will of God done. Hannah could not have known, at the beginning of her story, that her giving this little boy to serve at Shiloh would lead to a forward step in God's dealings with Israel. Samuel would be the king-maker who brought David to his position as model king for Israel. It all began with Hannah and her praying when in trouble.

Chapter 2

Honouring God

(1 Samuel 2:11–36)

Israel's sin was so offensive the priests who were leading the nation were about to be entirely removed by God. Shiloh, the central place of worship in the nation, would be destroyed. There was sin at Shiloh, the spiritual centre of the nation. God said: *'Those who honour me I will honour, but those who despise me will be disdained'* (2:30). When God's leaders are disgracing his name he is likely to take action.

God is dishonoured by religion which fails to lead to godliness. Although Eli wished to be a godly man and acted as friend to the young Samuel (2:11) and to Hannah (2:20), his weakness was his tolerance of his sons (2:12). He would rebuke them but would do nothing more (2;22–25). Despite a godly background his sons became wicked men (2:12), despising God's worship. Priests were permitted to have the breast and the right thigh of the sacrificed animal for themselves (see Leviticus 7:28–34). But the servant of Eli's sons would take whatever the sons liked rather than restrict himself to the portions that were allowed (2:13–14). Also (2:15) they would want the meat before the best portion had been sacrificed. They were dishonouring God by greed, violence (2:16–17) and (as we learn later) by their immorality.

Hannah and Samuel are a contrast to Eli and his sons. Samuel honours the Lord by sincere ministry to God (2:18).

His mother annually provides for the needs of Samuel, God's servant (2:19). Eli's prayers for her are heard by God (2:20–21), and she is rewarded.

Eli had apparently handed over much of his work to his sons. He would hear of the corruption of the worship at Shiloh (2:22) but would do little about it. He would complain to his sons (2:23–25) but would take no action. His sin was that of passivity. He was the most powerful person in Israel, for there was no king and he was the spiritual ruler of the land. He could have stepped in when he first heard of their corrupt ways. Yet he preferred to honour his sons. However, they did not honour Eli and would not obey what he asked (2:25).

The writer goes on (2:26–36) to tell us how God rewards or dishonours those who treat him in these different ways. Samuel was being progressively honoured by the Lord (2:26). Eli and his family were moving towards disaster.

1. **God honours us by speaking to us** and dishonours us by refusing to speak to us. A prophet comes (2:27) with a word from God. God had revealed himself to the nation (2:27). Soon he is speaking to Samuel but no longer speaking to Eli directly.

2. **God honours us by giving us honourable work**; he dishonours us by refusing to use us. God had chosen Eli's ancestor, Aaron, and had given him a ministry (2:28). Why should Eli get gain for himself in such a wicked way (2:29)? He too was profiting from the food that his sons obtained. The ways in which God had honoured his family would have continued for ever. Now Eli and his family were dishonouring God, and would reap a return according to the way they had lived (2:30).

3. **God honours us by meeting our needs**, and dishonours us by deprivation. *'I also gave your father's house all the offerings,'* says God (2:28). Part of the sacrifices were for the use of the priests. Now that would be lost.

4. **God honours us by allowing us to reap a good reputation**. Eli would be *'disdained'* (2:30).

5. **God honours us by giving us happiness within a family**,

but dishonours us by sending that which removes such happiness. God says to Eli *'I will cut off your arm'* (2:31), which means that Eli's own strength would soon fail. Soon he would be almost blind (3:2; 4:15). *'I will cut off the arm . . . of your father's house'* (2:31) means that a disaster would soon come upon the family. We shall read of the death of his sons (4:11) and of his daughter-in-law (4:20). About twenty years later the descendants of Eli were slaughtered by Saul (1 Samuel 22:17–20) and only Abiathar, Eli's descendants, escaped. A generation later still, Abiathar lost the privilege of the priesthood (1 Kings 2:27), and the privileges Eli had inherited were lost for ever. He would live to *'see the ruin of the house'*, the destruction of Shiloh. So frequently would tragedy strike Eli's family none would live to old age (2:32). God says (2:33): *'And any man belonging to you that I do not cut off from my altar will be weeping out his eyes and wearing out his strength and all the descendants of your family line shall die by the swords of men.'*[1] Soon Eli's sons shall die in one day (2:34). Another priest will be raised instead (2:35). The reference is to Zadok who in a future generation would replace the line of Eli (1 Kings) and would remain in the priesthood until the end of the Davidic kingship which as a political entity ended in the days of the exile to Babylon. Ultimately Jesus is the faithful priest who perfectly does all of God's will. The line of Zadok was an interim measure until the perfect priest should come. Until Jesus comes the Zadokite line would walk before the Davidic king. When the Saviour came he would be Davidic king and perfect High-Priest at the same time.

(6) **God honours us by giving us contentment** rather than deprivation and subservience. Eli's family would become so degraded that the remains of the family would be begging for financial assistance (a piece of silver), for food (a loaf of bread) and for employment (one of the priests' offices). The godly may suffer for a while. The ungodly may flourish. But in the long run, honouring God is rewarded. Honour comes to us, when honour is given to God.

Footnote

[1] I have followed the Hebrew reading of the Qumran manuscript, 4QSam[a], supported by Greek translations (see P.K. McCarter, *1 Samuel*, Doubleday, 1980, pp. 90–91).

Chapter 3

Hearing God's Voice
(1 Samuel 3:1–4:1a)

Sometimes God may go a long time without speaking both in the life of the people of God and in the life of an individual. In the days of Samuel, *'the word of the Lord was rare'* (3:1).

God does not have to speak to us in an audible voice as he did to Samuel, although that still happens. However, even without the audible voice what happened to Samuel is comparable to what happens to us when God speaks to us.

1. **It is possible to hear God's voice but not know it**. Sometimes when God is speaking to us we do not realise it. We can be restless, as when Samuel could get no sleep because the voice of God continued to come to him (3:2–8a). We might act strangely towards others, as when Samuel kept disturbing Eli. God's convictions might make us miserable. They might make us angry. Samuel was hearing the voice of God but did not realise it. It perplexed him, because he was not familiar with the voice of God coming to him in this way. *'The word of the Lord had not yet been revealed to him.'*

2. **It is possible for the true believer to cease to hear the voice of God**. Eli was a true believer, but in a bad state at the time we are considering. Samuel and Eli were both lying down in the tabernacle at Shiloh (3:2–3). When God spoke, he spoke only to Samuel (3:4–6). Samuel was not used to being spoken to in that way (3:7).

Eli was **not** hearing God's voice. Yet he had enough spiritual knowledge to know what was happening to Samuel. He was even able to give Samuel good advice (3:8–9). Eli was there and the message was about him (3:10–14) and yet God would not give the message to Eli. It is a high privilege to know that we are being spoken to by God. If God is pleased with us we are likely to be conscious of his voice, conscious of living fellowship with him. When God is displeased with us we are likely to discover he is speaking to others but not speaking to us. We may find that God is revealing to others things that we need to know. In the case of Eli we have some-one who had heard the voice of God in days gone by, but was not hearing God's voice at that particular time. Similarly we may find that God will talk about us, but will not talk to us.

When a person has known the Lord but at the present time in his life is distant from God, he may still know a lot. He may be able to give good advice. He can remember days when God blessed him and spoke to him. He recognizes when God is speaking to others. But it is a sad situation to be in. Hebrews says *'Today, if you hear His voice, do not harden your hearts....'* Some believers no longer hear God's voice. It happened to Saul (1 Samuel 28:5–6).

3. **It is possible to hear God's voice, know that one is hearing God's voice and want to know more of God's voice**. The third situation we find in this chapter, is that of Samuel after he has been helped by Eli. Then Samuel **knew** what was happening. Before this time the voice of God was not well-known to Samuel. He had not known the Lord speaking to him in this way. Something like this can happen to us. It may take us time before we realise what it means for us to be hearing from God.

Someone might want to ask 'is the modern way of hearing God's voice simply a matter of reading the Bible?' I answer as follows. The written Word of God is the greatest form of the Word of God, but there are other forms. God has other ways of speaking. The greatest way is to know we are being addressed through the Scriptures. But there can also be revelations in the midst of worship. There can be 'coinci-dences' where we know God is saying something to us. There can come convictions by the Spirit, intuitions, spiritual instincts or the direct impulses of the Spirit (see Acts 8:29), or the forbidding of the Spirit (see Acts 16:6, 7). A word from God may come through a dream or vision. All of these have to be thoroughly tested but the written Word of God does not have to be tested. It has been tested already a thousand times. Sometimes preaching will come to us with the forcefulness of a word from God. Sometimes the counsel of other Christians convicts us. Sometimes the voice of God comes amidst unusual circumstances.

Hearing the Bible by the Spirit is more than just reading. Even when we have the written Word of God we still need the Spirit. The Pharisees had the Old Testament and loved it but did not see Jesus in its pages. They had the Bible; they did not have the Spirit.

We need first then to ask God to speak to us. When he has spoken to us we need to press on to ask for more, as Samuel did. God often speaks in two phases. Sometimes he tells us a little bit and then waits for us to seek him to get more, to say *'Master speak, your servant is hearing.'* He called Samuel by name and then waited for Samuel to want more. He did the same to Daniel. Daniel knew something from God (Daniel 9:2) but had to seek for more (Daniel 9:3). It happened to all the prophets. The prophets received one phrase of revelation and then had to seek for more (1 Peter 1:10, 11). Then they got another phrase of revelation (1 Peter 1:12). It happens that way still.

When Samuel did hear God, there was a difficult task ahead of him (3:15–17) but he did what he knew he had to do (3:18). It was his obedience to what God was showing him that led to his receiving further words from God and that led to his ministry as spokesman for God (3:19–4:1a).

Chapter 4

Superstition

(1 Samuel 4:1b–10)

Eli's two sons, Hophni and Phineas, brought terrible corruption to the heart of the nation. Calamity was bound to fall upon Israel soon.

One day the nation goes out to battle against their old enemies, the Philistines. Israel is defeated and loses four thousand men (4:1b–2).

When we experience defeat we need to enquire into the cause. When Israel was defeated in so striking a manner it was natural for them to ask why. So the elders of the people asked *'Why has the* Lord *defeated us today before the Philistines?* (4:3a). They were right to ask the question, and they were right to attribute their defeat to the Lord. On previous occasions victory had been given them, sometimes quite miraculously. When they were right with God, they were victorious. When they sinned they experienced defeat.

However, spiritual understanding in Israel was at a low level. Their question was right, but they came up with an answer that was foolish. They decided that they needed to be more religious than ever before, and carry the ark of the Lord before them as they went into battle. They thought this would bring back their old spiritual power (4:3b).

When God's people fail they often increase their 'religiousness', but to do so does no good. The cause of the failure of Israel is the sin at Shiloh! Can they not see it? Apparently not. When the ark of the Lord is taken out to battle, Hophni and Phineas, the very men whose wickedness had brought such defeat upon the nation, are there alongside it (4:4). The ark will do no good, but the presence of Hophni and Phineas will invite calamity.

It was a move in the direction of religiousness. When the people of God sin, strangely we can intensify our religiousness to somehow 'make up for' the fact of our disobedience. (We recall the useless fasting of Isaiah 58:3 and the explanation of its uselessness in Isaiah 58:4.)

It was also a move in the direction of traditionalism. Israel had many years ago gone into battle with the ark in front of them and had been given great victory. It was present at the time of the conquest of Jericho (Joshua 3:6; 6:6). They thought that increased religion and a return to the traditions of the old days would somehow bring them victory against the Philistines.

This is religious superstition. Often people with little knowledge of God think that if they put their trust in some religious object, then all will be well and God will be with them. Superstition is when we put our trust in buildings or in religious objects or in 'holy' people, instead of dealing directly with God. There is only one thing that enables us to please God and get his victories. That is to deal with him directly, to find out his will for our life, and get on with pleasing him by direct obedience. If that is not done, no amount of religion or tradition will bring his blessing.

The people go forward with this strange combination. There with the army of Israel was the ark of God which symbolised God's holy presence. But they were totally unaware of the demands of God's holiness and there also with the ark were Hophni and Phineas. It is called the *'ark of the covenant'* (4:4). The covenant is the arrangement between Israel and God made at the time of Moses. God had said if they would obey his voice, they would be a holy nation (Exodus 19:5, 6). He had required that the summary of the law, the ten commandments, should be placed within the ark. Maybe it was there as they were carrying it. But if the law was inside the ark, Hophni and Phineas who had broken God's law in numerous ways were only a few yards away from the written law they had broken. They were marching into battle with a combination of sin and religiousness, with a combination of tradition and carelessness.

Such superstition was doomed from the start! God simply does not bless a combination of religious traditionalism with wickedness. It was of no value to use the ark as a kind of 'good luck charm'. People often use churches and ministers in this way, thinking that some kind of good will come merely by their connections with church or by getting a preacher to say a prayer for them. But the blessings of God come with direct faith in God and obedience to what he is asking. The kind of religiosity that falls into superstition is of no value at all and is quite deceptive.

The Israelites get very excited, very 'pentecostal', and shout great shouts of jubilance and expectation (4:5). But charismatic religiosity will not be blessed more than any other religiosity if there is sin in the camp. The Philistines hear about it and they are alarmed (4:6–9). The people of God and the pagans are as superstitious as each other! When the people of God are a long way from the LORD they are not much different from those who are totally without faith in the God of the Bible. The inevitable happens. The Israelites are defeated and *'the slaughter was very great'* (4:10).

Superstition does no good. It does not prevent the judgement of God. It deceives men and women because it makes them think that God is somehow nearer. But without a Saviour, without righteousness, superstition can only bring the wrath of God nearer.

The question they asked was the right one. *'Why has the LORD defeated us...?'* The true answer was, 'Because sin is at the heart of the nation, in Shiloh.' The next thing would have been to plead with Eli to remove his sons, and to plead with the LORD to return to them and have mercy upon them.

The same is true today. The way to know God is to face the facts of our sinfulness and call upon Jesus to cleanse us. Then God will come to us and give us victory over every kind of evil.

Chapter 5

Spiritual Laziness
(1 Samuel 4:1b–22)

Passivity in the things of God leads to disaster. This is one of the themes of this chapter and its surrounding narrative. It was Eli's passivity with regard to his sons that led the nation of Israel into chaos in the first place. When given warning by a prophet (2:27–35), he does not seem to have responded at all. When a further warning came through Samuel he said only *'He is the LORD; let him do what is good in his eyes'* (3:18). What a contrast Eli is with Joshua when something similar happened earlier in the story of the nation. When Israel was defeated in connection with the sin of Achan, Joshua *'tore his clothes and fell face down to the ground before the ark of the LORD'* (Joshua 7:6). The elders at the time of Joshua did the same and sprinkled dust on their heads as a mark of their intense distress. Joshua went to God with agonizing prayer (Joshua 7:7–9). But there is nothing like that in the story of Eli. 'Ah well', he says, 'He is the LORD; let him do what he likes!' His faith in the sovereignty of God leads him into complacency.

We notice too how different is the reaction of the Philistines compared to that of Israel. The Philistines are much more sensible!

1. **They want to know the facts**. When they learn about the ark, they say *'What's all this shouting?'* (4:6). They want to know what is happening and take the trouble to find out.

25

2. **They rightly assess the seriousness of the situation**. *'We're in trouble,'* they say (4:7).

3. **They are able to recognize a new situation**. They say *'Nothing like this has ever happened before'* (4:7).

4. **They respond with concern and resolution**. *'Woe unto us!'* they say. *'Who will deliver us . . . ?'* And they go on to weigh up their danger, *'These are the gods who struck the Egyptians with all kinds of plagues . . . '* (4:8). It is precisely this note that is so lacking in the Israelites. The Israelites, led by the elderly Eli, seem so complacent, so lacking in concern, when considered alongside these Philistines.

5. **The Philistines call the people to take strong action**. *'Be strong, Philistines! Be men, or you will be subject to the Hebrews, as they have been to you. Be men, and fight!'* (4:9). It is a call to energy and zeal. It is mixed with a certain amount of warning. It faces the fact that valiant and violent conflict will be needed.

So the Philistines won a victory. They responded sensibly to the situation they found themselves in. But this was precisely what the people of God should have done. If they had got hold of the realities of the situation they would have recognized how seriously God regarded the sin taking place in his sanctuary at Shiloh. If they had been thinking straight they would have said 'We are in trouble! God is angry with us'. They would have recognized that something had developed in Israel which required action. They would have called on God for mercy.

The people of God did not respond in this way but the Philistines did. It often happens that the people of the world are wiser in their generation than the people of the light (Luke 16:8). Worldly Philistines can be very practical! They look the situation straight in the eye and face the realities of what is happening around them. In their own way they can be wiser than the people of God.

The people of God, on the other hand, can be so religious that their religious ideas make them forget to face plain and straightforward facts. They have a high view of the sovereignty of God. 'He is the LORD; let him do what he likes,' they say. It is very sound theology! But it is not what the situation requires. The sins of Hophni and Phineas were arousing no alarm.

So when the Israelites marched into battle with the ark there was calamity in every way. The ark was lost (10:11a). Hophni and Phineas received their long-delayed judgement (4:11b). The terrible predictions and warnings that had been given by various prophets and servants of God began to be fulfilled. A messenger arrived (4:12). Eli was waiting for news of the battle. But he was still combining concern for the things of God with refusal to do what was needed. Did he think the ark would do any good? Apparently he was filled with foreboding; his heart was trembling (4:13a). When the messenger arrived the hopes of Shiloh were shattered and their worst fears confirmed (4:13b). Eli, now aged and blind, found out what was happening (4:14–17). When he got the news he knew it was the sign he had been told about (see 2:34). He himself died the same day (4:18). Other prophecies concerning his family also began to be fulfilled. His daughter-in-law died (4:19–20). Her son was named 'Ichabod', which means 'No glory' (4:21). Associated with the ark was the radiating presence of God with Israel. Now it was lost (4:22).

The judgement of God had been slow in coming. Warnings had been given along the way. Repentance might have averted the judgement. But Eli and the elders of the nation were not thinking spiritually. They felt that the presence of the ark would deliver them but they did not have the spiritual insight to draw attention to the wickedness at Shiloh. They did not have the kind of relationship with God that kept their eyes open to the real need of the hour. When the people of God are in such spiritual blindness, God may leave aside an entire generation and start somewhere else. So Eli and his family were abandoned. The sanctuary at Shiloh would never be used by God again. God started again with his people, beginning with Samuel. Possibilities of recovery were to be found in someone who could hear God's voice.

Chapter 6

The People With Two Gods
(1 Samuel 5:1–6:12)

The Philistines placed the ark in the temple of Dagon (5:1–2). They were ignorant people and thought the ark was itself Israel's God. They thought that if they adopted the God of Israel as their God also, he might do wonderful things for them.

But although they brought God into their temple, they did not put Dagon out! There are many people who think it is useful to have God on their side. In a way they want to honour God. They will go to church. They will say prayers. They will ask a pastor to bless a marriage or their new house. The kind of God they want is simply a God who will help them get their own way and win their own battles. They want God to be a servant to help them get things done, but they want to live their own lives and have their own views at the same time.

What is needed in the lives of such people is that they should discover God as the living God. Sometimes God does something that, if we only take notice, will get us to see that he is the living God. The Philistines got up the next morning and found their idol fallen on his face before the ark of the LORD (5:3a). God has a habit of knocking our idols down. But then we have a habit of putting our idols back up again, and this is what the Philistines did (5:3b). The next day the same thing had happened again (5:4), only now Dagon was without his head (a hint that he cannot rule) and without his

28

hands (a hint that he cannot to anything). The God of Israel is not simply another god to be put alongside others. He is not simply someone we can take into our lives to be helpful to us when we need him. He is the mighty living God who will knock all our idols down when he feels like it.

The Philistines got to know that God is the living God. But they were so ignorant of God that it led them to add one more superstition to all the others. From that point on they 'hopped' over the threshold of their temples (5:5). (The custom is mentioned again in Zephaniah 1:9.)

While they were trying to have their own idols alongside the living God there was no blessing in their lives. Devastation came in the form of a plague of rats (see 6:4–5), and the rats brought sickness (5:6).

In their own muddled way they sought to be right with God. They did not have any clear revelation or guidance and yet they came to some conclusions that were almost right.

1. **They came to see that they had to get right with God**. It had become obvious to them that the God of Israel could affect their lives and so now they wished to do something to be right with him. They recognized God's activity (5:7), and called a meeting to decide what to do (5:8a).

2. **They knew that what they had done was offensive to God, but could not find a way to please him**. In their ignorance they struggled to find a way of being right with God. Did the God of Israel not like sharing a temple with Dagon? Then they would take him elsewhere. They took the ark to Gath (5:8b) and then when that did not seem to help (5:9), they tried Ekron (5:10). But the people of Ekron did not like the idea at all and the move still did not seem to please the God of Israel (5:11–12). After seven months of experimentation they decided that God wanted his ark sent back (6:1–2). The question was – how should it be sent back?

All of this is typical of people who have come to the conclusion that God is real but do not know how to get to know God. They struggle to find a way of pleasing God, but our ways of trying to please God are not acceptable to him.

3. **They were right in thinking that something had to be done about their past offensiveness to God**. The God they had offended would not simply ignore what they had done. They felt that if they were to be reconciled to God some kind of sacrifice would be needed (6:3). It had to be a sacrifice for their sins, so they made some valuable gold gifts in the shape of the rats and the tumours that had been troubling them, so that it would be clear this was a gift to atone for the sin that had brought those particular judgements (6:4–6). They found a way of deciding whether the whole affair was simply coincidence and the ark went back to Israel (6:7–12).

In much of this their conscience and their religious instinct was right but hazy. They were right to think we cannot simply 'forget the past'. They were right to think that a sacrifice was needed before God would be reconciled to them. But they invented their own sacrifice, not knowing that God would provide a sacrifice of his own. The instinct many people have that a sacrifice for sin is needed is a right and true instinct. The truth is, God's sacrifice for sin is Jesus. God's law required sacrifices with blood in it. Only sacrifices which involved the shedding of blood were adequate to express what Jesus would one day do for sinners needing reconciliation with God. The Philistines were following the instincts of muddled consciences. When the light of the gospel came what they were looking for would be available in Jesus. He would be the sacrifice for sin that they needed but could not find.

Chapter 7

The Presence of God

(1 Samuel 6:13–7:1)

The ark of God was a symbol of the presence of God.

1. **The presence of God is a precious blessing**. God was offended at the Philistines' retaining the ark, for at this stage of history his presence was promised only to Israel. Only one people had the promise of the special presence of God. When we use the word 'presence' in this way, we mean his being present in blessing. Of course God is 'present' throughout the whole universe, but Israel was promised the special 'presence' of God in blessing. The promise continues in the revised and re-structured 'Israel', which is the Christian church.

2. **The presence of God brings joy**. The people of Beth-shemesh find that they are the ones to whom the ark, the symbol of God's presence, comes. They rejoice (6:13). The return of the ark holds out hope that God will return to Israel. The radiating, shining, presence of God had been with Israel in the shrine at Shiloh. That glory had departed and in the loss of the ark the symbol of God's presence had been lost also. Now the men of Bethshemesh see something that gives them hope that the presence of God will return.

The spiritual equivalent of the ark in the life of the church is the enjoyment of the presence of God. There are times in the life of the church when God seems specially present (see 1 Corinthians 14:25). It is always an occasion of great joy to the church of Jesus when 'the ark comes back' and God's presence in unusual blessing is experienced. This is what we call 'revival'.

3. **The presence of God demands consecration**. It is a high privilege to have the presence of God with us. It demands some kind of response. The people of Bethshemesh immediately used the wood of the cart and the cows (6:14–15) to make 'burnt offerings' (speaking of total dedication to God) and 'sacrifices' (speaking of renewed fellowship). It was a dedication witnessed by the Philistines who were nearby watching all that was going on (6:16). We are told the details of what the Philistines had offered to the LORD (6:17–18a; NASV is closer to the Hebrew than the NIV) and we read of the large stone that was remembered many years later in the days of the author or compiler of 1 and 2 Samuel. The story of the way in which God had protected his ark and virtually forced the Philistines to return it was remembered for many years to come (6:18b). Despite the folly of the Israelites in using the ark superstitiously, God still had mercy on them and made his own arrangements to get the ark returned. The Israelites got their ark back by God's mercy, not by their own efforts or deservings. This point was memorialised as a permanent witness to God's grace. We too easily forget God's grace and if we are sensible will take some effort to *'keep ourselves in the love of God'* (Jude 21). Even when we are faithless, God remains faithful.

4. **The presence of God is dangerous**. It is his holy presence. The death of the men of Bethshemesh (6:19a) seems harsh to the modern reader. *'He struck seventy among the people, fifty chief men.'* [1] But it must be remembered that the ark was meant to be kept in a shrine. Nothing but calamity had come upon Israel's misuse of it. It spoke of the utter purity and holiness of God. No-one was normally allowed even to see it. Certainly no-one was allowed to look inside it. For within the holy ark of God was the law, including its sharpest and most penetrating demand *'You shall not covet.'* It is a law no-one can keep (if the tenth commandment is taken into consideration). If one tries to look directly at the holiness of God, represented by the tenth command which requires that we

shall not even desire any sin whatsoever, nothing but death can be the result. The presence of God is his holy presence. If we try to look at him directly, there is no place of safety for the sinner. The law of Moses demanded that the way into the holy presence of God should be by atoning blood. The men of Bethshemesh failed to realise that there can be nothing but the severest judgement if there is any attempt to approach God without atoning blood. It grieved the people (6:19b) and made them realise the holiness of God more than ever (6:20). They were afraid to have the presence of God – even in symbolic form – so near and asked that the ark should be taken to Kiriath Jearim (6:21–7:1).

The story of the men of Bethshemesh is a permanent reminder that our curiosity needs to be controlled when we come to deal with the things of God. It is with reason that Paul cries out *'O the depth of the wealth, wisdom and knowledge in God! How unsearchable are His judgements!'* To look directly at the holiness of God was forbidden by the law itself (Numbers 4:20). God cannot be approached directly. *'Who is able to stand before the LORD, this holy God?'* they said. They were even hoping that God would leave them. *'And to whom shall He go away from us so as to relieve us of His presence?'* (the Hebrew has this sense).

The fact is we are invited to draw near to God with boldness only by the blood of sacrifice. At the same time as we come to God we recall that God is a consuming fire (Hebrews 4:16; 12:29). It is only the blood of Jesus that enables us to draw near to God. Only in that way do we get to the joys of his presence.

Footnote

[1] This is probably the correct translation rather than *'fifty thousand men'*. A village such as Bethshemesh would not have 50,000 men in it, and the Hebrew word *'eleph'* sometimes means 'chief of a thousand' or 'chief man'.

Chapter 8

Rebuilding a Nation

(1 Samuel 7:2–17)

After a time of stagnation in the story of Israel, Samuel was able to bring spiritual restoration to the people of Israel.

1. **God gave the nation a chance for renewal and restoration**. It seems to have been the Philistine oppression of Israel that brought the people to the point where they were lamenting after the Lord (17:2). This had often happened, as Samuel mentions later (1 Samuel 12:9–11). A time of crisis in the nation is likely to be a time of seeking the Lord. But the servants of God have to take action and exploit such a situation for God, as Samuel did. Samuel takes advantage of this movement among the people and seeks to consolidate it into a real forward step in the relationship between God and the nation.

2. **This restoration requires thorough repentance**. He says *'If you are returning to the Lord ... remove the foreign gods...'* (7:3). A superficial repentance will do no good. An emotional repentance will achieve nothing. There must be a true putting away of idols if God is to bless and restore the nation. The people heed him and actually turn from their national sins of idolatry and give themselves to the Lord alone (7:4). Modern nations need to do the same. Perhaps the national sins may not be 'Ashtoroth' (statues of a female goddess); the local idols may be the sins of financial greed and spiritual laziness. But the principles are the same.

Restoration involved Samuel's intercession. Samuel

summons the people to Mizpah and promises to intercede for them (7:5). The people repent of their idolatrous ways (7:6). The pouring out of water seems to have been a way of expressing the need for cleansing. It was as though the people were saying 'We have sinned and need to be washed clean'. The fasting was an expression of seriousness. The eating of food was given up in order to give time to prayer and concentrating on seeking restoration and God's blessing. After that Samuel 'judges' the people; that is to say, he rules over them, guides them, instructs them in the ways of God and counsels them in situations of perplexity.

3. **The time of restoration was soon tested**. Soon after this spiritual restoration there comes a time of testing. Once again, as often had happened before, the Philistines attack (7:7a). It was viciously timed. The devil knows how to send 'an evil day', a time when the attack of the enemies of God's people seems to catch them at their weakest. For the Philistines, the chance to invade at the time of an unarmed religious assembly was too great to be missed.

The people pass God's test by responding in faith. The people of Israel are alarmed (7:7b) but put their trust in the intercession of Samuel (7:8). He in turn as their intercessor and priest offers a lamb in sacrifice (7:9). It is a sacrifice that speaks of consecration to God. At the same time as he sacrifices the lamb the Philistines attack. It is a spiritual principle fulfilled in Jesus. When attacked by Satan the Christian has an intercessor, someone who prays that they might be kept from the evil one (John 17:15). He does his interceding because he is the Righteous One (1 John 2:2) and reigns at the right hand of the Father with a perfect righteousness which entitles him to have all his prayers answered.

4. **True amendment of life brought God's deliverance in a way that was wonderful in its method and in its timing**. Here are a people newly dedicated to God, yet their dedication does not release them from being attacked by Philistines. Far from it! It might have seemed quite impossible for God to protect Israel. They were defenceless, having been caught in the middle of a meeting for repentance over their idolatrous

35

ways. They would not have come to Mizpah in any way armed for battle against the Philistines. It seemed to be a situation where total slaughter of the Israelites was inevitable. But if the situation was desperate God was capable of doing something dramatic. As the Philistines invaded a terrifying thunderstorm took place (7:10) which because of its violence and because it took place at the very point the Philistines were attacking, threw them into extreme panic. All the Israelites had to do was to rush down upon them, perhaps even picking up weapons abandoned by the Philistines, and utterly defeat them (7:11).

5. **Restoration led to long-term consolidation**. What had happened led into a period of Israel's history where the people were given victory and dominance over their enemies and a time of peace. It did not last indefinitely (as the next chapter of 1 Samuel shows) but while it lasted it was a significant and prosperous time in Israel's history.

At the beginning of this time Samuel marked the occasion when God had rescued the people by putting up a memorial stone and naming the place Ebenezer *'stone of help'* (7:12). We are meant to learn God's ways. God's rescuings are something he is likely to do again and again. When we have been delivered from a crisis once we must remember that the same God is able to deliver us again. One way of encouraging ourselves to do this is to make careful note of his deliverances and resolve not to forget them.

It was a minor turning point in the history of Israel. The Philistines were subdued (7:13), cities were restored to Israel (7:14). Samuel was established as the ruler of Israel for many years (7:15). He diligently watched over the affairs of the nation (7:16) attending different parts of the country personally (7:16), but making his home at Ramah his headquarters (7:17). Samuel took practical steps to stay in touch with the entire nation. His circuits around the land gave the people easy access to him and enabled him to truly know the situation of his people. For at least a generation such a ministry led the nation into the blessings of God.

Chapter 9

Finding a Leader
(1 Samuel 8:1–22)

As Samuel got older the need of a new leadership began to be obvious. Here is a major question: **how is blessing perpetuated once God has given it?** The ministry of Samuel had been a great time of peace and pastoral supervision. But what will happen now? Once again, the sons of a national leader regarded themselves as candidates for leadership. **It is the easy way to think that leadership can simply be inherited**. Eli's sons had done damage to the worship of Israel. Now the pattern seems as if it might repeat itself; Samuel's sons seek to step into the father's position. They start assisting him in the southern part of the kingdom where Beersheba was to be found (8:1–2). They do not seem to have been quite so wicked as Hophni and Phineas but still they were corrupt and more concerned about personal gain than about spirituality. This is typical of people who come into office without being called by God. They were grandchildren of the godly Hannah and children of the godly Samuel but grace is not inherited via the family line and Samuel's two sons like Eli's two sons were corrupt (8:3).

How then can good leadership be found? The people of Israel were conscious of the ways of the surrounding nations. They were wanting the kind of powerful protection a king could provide. Samuel's age and his corrupt sons gave the people an argument for what they really wanted which was to have a king and so be like the surrounding nations (8:4–5). This too is also trying to perpetuate blessing by physical descent, for it somehow hopes that one good king will be succeeded by an equally good son.

Samuel takes this as a rejection of his leadership (8:6), but handles his feelings of rejection by taking the matter to God in prayer. God tells him to accept their request but at the same time says that they are really rejecting the kingship of God (8:7).

The people's desire is a piece of worldliness. The wish for a king comes from seeing what happens in the surrounding world and wanting to be like it. They are concerned about how to handle enemies, and this is the best they can think of. **The true answer was to look to God**. In days gone by they had cried to God and God had sent them deliverers in a remarkable way. There had been the remarkable deliverance at Ebenezer, and the memorial stone was still there to remind them of it (1 Samuel 7:10–12).

The people's desire is trust in military might. A king would be a soldier protecting the nation by his wars and his armies. It was the rise of enemies of Israel that made them want a protector (see Samuel's words in 12:12).

The rejection of God shows itself in rejection of God's servant (8:8). They forgot the many times God had intervened. They forgot that their being overrun by enemies was the result of turning to other gods. They forgot what Samuel had done for them some years before. All they could see was the rise of powerful enemies such as Nahash of the Ammonites (see 12:12).

The modern church often has similar questions, and often follows worldly ways in seeking leadership. Pride and empire-building often creep in and do great damage to the people of God. What it comes to is this; do we want 'official' leadership, 'committee' leadership, and 'management principles', or do we want God-given men and women raised up for the hour? It is important to have some recognizable order but the danger is that sheer worldliness will creep in, so that we think we can 'arrange' a good system.

God punished Israel by giving them what they wanted. Sometimes if we are insistent on going our own way God administers a powerful rebuke by giving us our desires.

Samuel is told to warn them of the implications of kingship. It will involve (i) compulsory service of the king – a conscription into national service (8:11–13), (ii) appropriation of property for royal use (8:14), (iii) an additional royal tithe (8:15), (iv) loss of employees because of the king's demands (8:16), (v) taxation or appropriation of wealth in the form of animals (8:16, 17a), and (vi) reduced personal liberty (*'you shall be his servants,'* 8:17b). Also Samuel predicts that kingship would lead to eventual distress but the situation would be one which could not be reversed and cries of distress would not be heard (8:18).

All this was a serious warning, but the people are not convinced and insist on having a king (8:19–20). Samuel hears it all, shares it with God in prayer, is instructed to accede to their request and tells them to go back to their cities as he prepares to set up kingship for them as they have requested (8:21–22).

What was needed was further calling upon God as had happened in the past, so that God would raise up for them new leaders. This was God's appointed way. Even if they got a good king, could they guarantee his son's suitability for the next generation? When Jesus came he was a directly-given leader and Saviour. No committee chose him. Apostolic leadership is similar. It comes *'not from people ... not through people, but through Jesus Christ'* (Galatians 1:1).

We must learn to recognize men and women that God raises up. Our systems of our own devising for finding leaders, do not work in the church of Jesus Christ.

We must seek God as the situation requires, and be careful about systems that give leaders to the church in a worldly way. No worker should be in God's work unless he is manifestly suited to what he is doing. As Paul said of deacons, *'Let them also be tested ... if they prove themselves blameless let them serve'* (1 Timothy 3:10). By getting an inherited kingship the need to seek God generation by generation was being side-stepped! God rebukes them by giving them what they want! Better is Jesus' way: *'Request ... from the Lord ... that he may thrust out workers ... '* (Matthew 9:38).

Chapter 10

Exaltation Without Manipulation
(1 Samuel 9:1–10:1)

Saul is famous for ruining his life. There came a time when he was abandoned by God for the remainder of his earthly life. God refused to speak to him. He lost his calling.

Yet in 1 Samuel 9 we discover how well he started out. Saul was promoted to become the first king of Israel. Any kind of true exaltation comes from God. 1 Samuel 9 is the story of how exaltation came for Saul.

It was a case of gifts and calling coming together. Saul had the gifts. He was a good choice for a king. His father was a man of standing (that is, 'upper class', 'wealthy') (1 Samuel 19:1). He had a good background with a respectable genealogy (9:2). He was tall (9:3), and impressive. So he had the background appropriate for a king.

Yet when we first meet him he is diligently getting on with the calling he was in at the time. Eventually God would take him from looking for donkeys to looking after God's kingdom.

1. **Saul was not wanting this promotion too much**. Promotion did not come for Saul by massive struggles or manipulation. Indeed he would have been rather surprised if you had told him he was to be king. He was not looking for a kingdom. He was getting on with the mundane, boring job of finding his father's asses. If you had asked him what his ambition was he might have answered: to be a successful farmer. He seems not to have been pushing for anything higher than

that. Donkeys were lost. Saul was willing to look for them. He was a young man obeying his father (9:3–4), and taking a lot of trouble to do so (9:4–5).

Jesus was like that. He did not exalt himself. He did not decide to be a great high-priest for the human race. We are told that Christ did not take the glory of being high-priest upon himself. He was called to it by God. God said to him, I am calling you to be the Saviour of the world (see Hebrews 5:5).

So Saul was going about his ordinary work. He was diligent, capable. If he was quietly ambitious, he was not overbearingly so.

2. **God has a habit of doing the unexpected for those who are faithful**. Saul was looking for asses; he had no interest in looking for the prophet Samuel. He did not suggest seeing Samuel, and he actually put obstacles in the way when it was suggested he do so (9:5–7).

When Saul was totally free from manipulating, suddenly a lot of 'coincidences' all begin happening at once. It was traditional to ask a prophet for advice when you were looking for something lost, and to give some kind of contribution. Saul has not come prepared for that. But the servant 'happens' to have a silver shekel with him. Some girls just 'happen' to know exactly where Samuel is (9:7–11). Samuel just 'happens' to be in town that very day (9:12). It just 'happens' to be the right time to find him (9:13). When they go into town Samuel is the first person they meet (9:14). When the time for our exaltation has come we shall not have to manipulate it. God will do it! Everything will fit. We shall know that we are in the will of God.

3. **When you are being exalted God works at both ends**. God was not only working in Saul to come to Samuel, he was working in Samuel to be ready for Saul. This is the way it is when God is truly at work. He brings together the gifted person and the place when he will use his gifts. Samuel was walking in the Spirit. God was able to speak to him. He knew ahead of the time that Saul would be coming (9:15–16). When

Saul appears God speaks to Samuel at that very time also (9:17). God was leading step by step.

4. **When we are being exalted, God will take care of all of our concerns**. What would Saul be especially concerned about at this precise moment? He would be worried about the donkeys. At the key moment when Saul is meeting Samuel and being invited to join the prophet, he is told that the practical matter is taken care of. 'Don't worry about the donkeys', says Samuel.

Saul is overwhelmed. He was not seeking to be king! He feels insignificant (9:21). But Samuel treats him as an honoured guest (9:22–24), talks with him all night (9:25), and then just before he is about to leave tells Saul he will go with him some of the way (9:26). On the edge of town he sends the servant ahead and quietly and secretly anoints Saul as the first king of Israel (9:27–10:1).

God has made the entire human race for glory and honour (Psalm 8). The human race was made in the image of God, made to be admired. But all have sinned and lack the glory of God (Romans 3:23). Man has fallen from God's original plan. Yet it seems as if we all want our glory back but want it back by wrong means. We all feel strongly about what others think of us. We care about our reputation and self-esteem more than we like to admit. We desire praise, self-esteem, a good self-image, honour from others.

It is not entirely wrong to want to be exalted. God wants to 'glorify' us. The children of God in glory will have visible honour. Holiness will radiate out of them visibly.

But this honour and glory has to come from God. It is in this matter that Saul begins well. Take glory for yourself prematurely and you are making a big mistake. The secret of getting glory is to get it from God, and God alone. What God will do for you – in your own little way – is to make you a king. He will give you an area of life where you 'reign with Christ' and are much used by him. But it has to come from God, not from oneself.

Chapter 11

The Marks of Spirituality
(1 Samuel 10:2–11:15)

Three things were on Saul's mind at the time of his being chosen as Israel's first king. There was his need to find the asses. Then there was Saul's material and financial need. Earlier in the story he had been concerned about having no silver with him (9:7) and his servant had apparently given away what he had (9:8). Thirdly, there was the question whether Saul would have the ability and prowess to do the work of a king. These three matters are immediately cared for by God.

1. **God shows Saul that he is able to take care of his practical concerns**. Almost immediately something happens that shows Saul that God is well able to find the asses (10:2). Saul meets someone who tells him the asses are found.

2. **God shows Saul that his material and physical well-being is also supervised by God**. They meet men with abundant supplies of food and wine (10:3), some of which will be given to Saul and will meet his needs (10:4).

3. **God shows that his Spirit is able to give unusual powers and that he will be given whatever he needs for him to be king**. He is to go on a little further and will meet a group of prophets – men trained by Samuel in ministry and in charismatic worship (10:5). When he meets them the Spirit will come upon Saul and he will be caught up in spiritual ecstasy and praise (which is what 'prophesy' means here) (10:6).

These three signs will show him that all his needs and concerns will be met. He can do whatever is in his heart. He will not need special guidance all the time but will need to get on with whatever tasks present themselves for his attention (10:7). Soon Samuel will give him further guidance (10:8).

Immediately after this word of advice from Samuel, Saul becomes a 'new man'. Saul is already a believing man. What is happening here is not his 'conversion' but his being empowered by the Holy Spirit to do the work of a king in accordance with God's call (10:9). The three promised assurances come to pass immediately (10:9). One of them is described in detail (10:10–12).

The new king is a spiritual young man at the beginning and immediately shows some signs of God-given maturity and wisdom.

1. **He has learned to control his tongue** (10:13–16). He soon goes back to report to his uncle. It would be natural for him to boast of his new call but he has the wisdom not to do so.

2. **He has the wisdom to let his call work out without manipulation**. He simply lets God's programme take its course. Samuel calls the people to Mizpeh (10:17), reminds them of their sinful insistence on having their own way (10:18–19a), and calls them to a meeting in which a king will be found for them (10:19b). By a process of casting lots, the tribe of Benjamin is chosen as the tribe which will provide the king, then the family of the Matrites, and eventually the lot focuses on Saul. He has done nothing to promote himself and has actually taken positive steps not to be around during this time (10:20–21). Further prayer and seeking the Lord is needed to find him (10:22).

All of this means that Saul has continued letting God work out his future for him and has taken no steps to manipulate himself into the position of being king. God has done it all for him.

Yet when the final decision has become clear, it is obvious that Saul is appropriate for the task God has called him to. He has the stature and the bearing that is appropriate for a king (10:23). His position is clear from God and is confirmed by the people (10:24). Saul need never have any doubts about the matter. It is God who has put him into the position of being king.

3. **From the very beginning he faces the need of a forgiving spirit**. Samuel instructs the people (10:25a). Everyone goes back home from Mizpah and the kingship has been peacefully settled (10:25b). Bodyguards and supporters accompany Saul (10:26). However, a few troublemakers violently disliked Saul and his being king. Saul had the wisdom and spirituality to treat them in a peaceable way (10:27).

Soon the opportunity to get his revenge on the troublemakers presented itself. Nahash the Ammonite started mustering his forces ready to attack Jabesh-Gilead (11:1). The people were ready to surrender (11:1b). Nahash agrees on condition that the people become incapacitated for any kind of rebellion and that Israel is disgraced by its inability to do anything about it (11:2). The people ask for time (11:3) and begin looking for help (11:4). Saul gets to hear about it (11:5) and is empowered by the Spirit (11:6). He gathers the nation together boldly (11:7–8), tells the people of Jabesh-Gilead what to do (11:9–10), and the next day the Ammonites are thoroughly defeated (11:11). It is this victory that demonstrates irrefutably the God-given calling and ability of the new king, and so Saul is in a position to take revenge on those who had disparaged him (11:12). But he again confirms that he has a forgiving spirit (11:13). All of this demonstrates Saul's calling, and his kingship is confirmed yet again (11:14–15).

4. **The good beginning required persistence if it was to lead to full blessing for Saul**. God rewarded his forgiving attitudes by giving him a further confirmation of his calling, without his having to act in violence or in self-vindication. Saul has begun well. When in later chapters we find Saul becoming full of violence and hostility towards David, we must not forget that he began well. The day was to come when his disobedience ruined his life. But reward and ministry can be lost. John said '*Look to yourselves so that we do not lose what you have*

worked for but may win a full reward' (2 John 8). It is he that endures to the end who is kept safe and receives the reward for having served God.

Chapter 12

Getting a New Start
(1 Samuel 12:1–25)

Have you ever done something which you then bitterly regretted? Israel had rejected God as their king. It might seem that they had stepped out of the purpose of God for ever.

But even when the people of God have badly fallen there is the possibility of recovery.

If they are to experience a fresh start they must be convinced that what they did was wicked. Samuel points out (1) **that they got their own way**. Having a king was not God's idea, it was not Samuel's idea, it was their own idea. They have exactly what they wanted. They now have a king (12:1–2a).

He moves on to emphasize (2) **the seriousness of their having rejected him**. When God's people drift from him they treat his servants badly. Although it was God rather than Samuel whose kingship they had rejected, nevertheless they had not appreciated the fact that God had given them a good leader in Samuel. He had been their leader for a long time (12:2b). During that long time he had never exploited them (12:3–4). Both the LORD and his representative, his anointed king, Saul, are witnesses to his integrity (12:5). They will not be able to say that they chose a king because of the failure of the one God had given them, Samuel himself.

Next Samuel proceeds to point out (3) **that God has been entirely faithful to them**. Their sin was a failure of faith in him.

He had worked many 'righteous acts' to bring the nation into being (12:6–7) and then continued to perform righteous acts throughout their history (12:8). They had cried for help in Egypt (12:9) but then sinned (12:10). They cried for help again (12:11). The same event happened again and again. Sin brought calamity; repentance brought deliverance. Each time they cried for help God sent them deliverers (12:10–11). Then came the time when instead of turning to the LORD they wanted a king instead. When Nahash of the Ammonites was threatening them, they broke the pattern of what they had done before and instead of calling upon the LORD, they asked for a deliverer like the ones the nations had, an earthly king (12:12). That, says Samuel, is what they now have (12:13).

Samuel regards the recent history as part of the sinfulness and rebelliousness of Israel. But, says the prophet, (4) **God is willing to allow the people to start from afresh** as though their rebellion had not taken place at all. This is often what God does when we sin. He forgives us and then can pick up with us no matter what we have done. Again and again he gives us fresh opportunities. We sooner or later learn the folly of getting out of God's will.

Samuel says that if from that time they will *'fear the LORD and serve and obey him'*, if they will not rebel further against his commands, all will be well and their relationship with the LORD will pick up as if their sin had never taken place. If they sin, they will experience God's hostility. But there is one condition to all of this: they must see the sinfulness of what they had done. If they will confess that what they did in rejecting God's kingship was sinful, God will forgive their sin and will pick up with them again.

Samuel is eager that they should truly and thoroughly admit how wrongly they have behaved. He proposes to ask God to do something that will convince them. It is harvest time (12:16–17a), a dry time of the year. Samuel prays that it will rain (12:17b), and God dramatically answers (12:18).

As a result the people are convinced by what Samuel has been saying and confess their sins. They request Samuel to continue to be an intercessor (12:19). Samuel now presses home the message he had put to them before. If they will obey the Lord from this point, all will be well (12:20–21). There is another reason why God is reluctant to ever reject his people. He has chosen them and his reputation is bound up with what happens to them. If he rejects them, his power to keep and to restore is slandered and despised. The LORD will therefore not reject them (12:22). Samuel will continue to be their intercessor (12:23). But God is asking them to serve him faithfully, in gratitude towards him (12:24). If they persist in rebellion, further disaster will yet come upon them and their king (12:25).

God can be generous to us in this way because Jesus died for us. And this was true even of Old Testament believers. The death of Jesus works backwards and forwards in time. Even Old Testament believers were forgiven in the light of what God would do upon the cross. This is the point of Romans 3:25 (*'because of the passing over of sins committed in the past'*).

The promise of the gospel is: I will be merciful to their iniquities, and I will no more remember their sins. Amazingly, God can even accommodate himself to what you did and somehow those sins are turned around and they even may be taken up into the purpose of God. The sin of Jonah led to some pagan sailors being blessed (Jonah 1:16), although what he did was wicked and he was severely chastised for it. The wicked acts of men in crucifying Jesus were God's way of bringing salvation to the world. God often says to us: acknowledge what you did. I will forgive it. I will overrule it and incorporate it into my present will for your life. Jesus died for those sins. Hand yourself over to me and let me lead you from this time. But, says God, if you exploit my grace again, I can sweep you away. God is free. He does not have to give another chance in this way. But he often does. He has done it for me; he will do it for you. Only acknowledge what you did and he will start again with you.

Chapter 13

Unbelief

(1 Samuel 13:1–10)

King Saul began his kingship well. He had all the signs of spirituality and was divinely equipped for the ministry of kingship that God had given to him. This picture, however, decisively changes in 1 Samuel 13. One must remember that the narrator is only picking out certain highlights of the story. This story comes in because it was the decisive point at which Saul lost the possibility of a dynasty of kings that would have lasted for ever. One does not have to think that his rejection came only because of one incident. It is likely that Saul had steadily become disobedient and that this story is included simply because it was a decisive occasion.

The text begins with a note concerning Saul. *'Saul was thirty years old when he became king and he reigned over Israel for forty-two years'* (13:1). There are some numbers missing in the Hebrew manuscripts and no-one knows what was there originally. The New International Version is as good a reading as any and has the support of Acts 13:21.

We note (1) **the occasion of Saul's disobedience**. Saul's major task was to put down the Philistines. The story tells of an occasion when Saul formed two regiments of soldiers for himself and for Jonathan. He was feeling quite confident and had sent other soldiers home (13:2). Then Jonathan, with the smaller group of soldiers, showed great daring in making an attack on a Philistine 'garrison' (13:3a) (or the Hebrew word might mean 'monument' or 'administrator', which would explain why the Philistines were more than usually affronted). The Philistines are aroused. Suddenly there is trouble in the land. Saul needs to get back the soldiers who had gone home. He summons the whole nation to join in the conflict against the Philistines (13:3b). The nation is told that Saul had attacked the Philistines; Jonathan was acting on his behalf. The people were summoned to assemble at Gilgal ready for battle (13:4).

The Philistines also prepare for battle (13:5) and the Israelites are fearful. Some are hiding wherever they can (13:6). Some are crossing the river Jordan to an area they think is safer (13:7a). Those who were with Saul were terrified (13:7b) and greatly reduced in number.

Apparently there was an arrangement similar to the one mentioned in 1 Samuel 10:8. Samuel had promised to come to consecrate the army to God. He had said in effect 'Meet me at Gilgal and wait for seven days. Then I shall offer whole burnt offerings to consecrate ourselves to the Lord, and peace offerings to symbolise our happy relationship to God. We shall be looking to God to bless us in our time of need.' (This cannot be the **same** occasion as is mentioned in 10:8, although 1 Samuel 10:8 shows us that what we have here has been done by Samuel before. 1 Samuel 13:8 is telling us that Samuel had made an arrangement similar to the one in 10:8.) But now Saul is getting panicky. **What led Saul into disobedience was a crisis of faith. He was tested as to whether he would keep calm and simply go on believing**. Faith has two phases to it. What one could call 'initial faith' is the first time anyone ever believes. It immediately brings us into salvation because any faith in Jesus or (in Old Testament days) in the promises of God, introduces us into the blessings of Jesus' salvation. But saving faith becomes what one can call 'diligent faith' or 'continuous faith' or 'applied faith'. We are to go on believing. The measure of blessing we are going to get will depend on whether we apply our faith. When some crisis comes, will you apply your faith? A crisis is a test of whether you will persist in faith. We must take care that we do not lapse from faith and fail to experience the blessings of God as the living

God (see Hebrews 3:12). Sooner or later, to every Christian, something will come which will challenge whether we shall persist in believing. Jude verse 5 says *'The Lord having saved his people out of Egypt destroyed those who did not believe in the second phase.'* Saul has been a great believer so far but will he be obedient now? He has been told to wait at Gilgal and do nothing until Samuel comes (similar to 10:8).

There are several aspects to the crisis. **There is temptation because of reduced numbers**. The men begin to scatter (13:8). Saul is worried and says 'I will have to do something before Samuel gets here, because my army is leaving me.' Before God moves in a mighty way there can be a dwindling of numbers. Remember Gideon's army (Judges 7)? Remember John 6:66–67? Numbers are important but obedience is even more important. In 1 Samuel 14 the Philistines are defeated as the result of the faith of only two men, Jonathan and his armour-bearer!

Another aspect to the matter is the **delayed speed at which things were happening**. *'Samuel did not come'* (13:8). We all have to be taught how to be patient. Saul is eager that Samuel should come quickly. Then foolishly he does something he should not have done and acts the part of a priest in offering sacrifice (13:9). Actually it was just after Saul had taken things into his own hands that Samuel arrived (13:10). Saul did not have the patience to wait until the last moment. Foolishly he lapsed in faith just a few minutes before God's answer came. He started sinning and moved into great disobedience. God is not unsympathetic to our needs. He gives grace **in the time of need**. This is what Saul would not believe. God does not come to our rescue before we really need it. So often our faith is challenged and the question is, will we believe that God will come to our help **in time**?

Will we continue in faith? Will we trust that God will come as the living God, as the God who keeps his promises and always rescues us in time?

Chapter 14

Saul Loses a Kingdom

(1 Samuel 13:8–15a)

We are still observing (1) **the occasion of Saul's disobedience** (see page 51). The situation was very threatening. Saul's army was deserting him (13:8); the Philistines were arriving. So Saul took a disastrous step which damaged his life. He offered the sacrifice to inaugurate the battle-campaign (13:9).

We consider next (2) **the form of his disobedience**. His sin consisted of pride of office. He felt he was the king and could do anything now. When we feel our own power and authority, we are in danger of stepping out of our calling, over-stepping the limits of what is right for us.

One particular aspect of the matter is that Saul was intruding into the rights of a spiritual leader. Samuel as a priest and a prophet had the prerogative of offering the sacrifice. He was of the tribe of Levi. Saul was a king, of the tribe of Benjamin. It was a civic ruler pushing himself into the rights of 'the church' (to use New Testament language) or (to be more exact) into the rights of the spiritual side of the leadership of Israel. Saul had no right to do this. To apply the lesson in New Testament language – it was the state interfering with the church. Officials of the state have no power in the church's internal affairs. Saul as the king had no right to steal the privileges of the priesthood. The king could not be a priest. The priests of the tribe of Levi were never able to become kings. The kings were not allowed into the 'holy of holies' of the tabernacle or temple. Here is the king saying to the prophet and priest, 'you would not come so I did it'. He pushes himself into an area where he has no authority. When civic leaders push themselves into religious officialdom, they corrupt the faith of the nation. They are usually concerned for a religion that has no repentance in it. Saul has no great regard for God. He simply feels that the ritual must be finished as speedily as possible so as to get on with the battle! State leaders who push themselves into direct spiritual work generally (there are exceptions), want 'religion' on their side – and they want nothing more. I recall a country which called upon the churches to support its foreign policy by holding a day of prayer for its success! The state assumed its policy was right and wanted 'religious' people to support it.

God feels very strongly about interference with his worship. Saul shows a lot of arrogant high-handedness towards God's spiritual leader. He more or less blames him for not arriving on time. He demands that God should come at Saul's convenience. Saul needed him! The truth of the matter is that God's timing is always for his own glory, but man's timing is generally planned to make him feel self-assured. Saul was trying to make himself feel secure. He wanted everything right so that he would feel safe. God's timing makes us feel insecure in ourselves and we have to look to God for our security. Saul feels no guilt at what he had done and greets Samuel with great confidence and great ignorance (13:10).

We come then to consider (3) **the consequences of Saul's sin**. Samuel rebukes him (13:11) and listens for his answer. If Saul had immediately confessed his folly things might have been different. If Saul had come out into the open with God, all would have been well. If he had said 'Samuel, I realise I did something foolish. I should not have done what I just did', maybe things would have been forgiven. But Saul does not say anything like that. He is confident, self-righteous, defensive (13:11b), pretending he had no choice (13:12). Samuel's analysis is different. Saul had been foolish and disobedient (13:13), so he has forfeited part of the plan of God for his life. God's plan was that he should be the founder of a dynasty.

'The LORD would have established your kingdom for ever' (13:13) but now the dynasty is to be given to someone else (13:14–15a).

Saul's disobedience paved the way for further disobedience. Saul's story from this point on is the story of steady decline. He goes from bad to worse. Yet he did not lose everything at precisely this point. He still could have sought God's forgiveness and restoration. But disobedience on one occasion makes it easier for there to be disobedience on another occasion. The next time it is easier to disobey.

It did not have to happen that way. Have you panicked in a crisis? Did you do something you should not have done? It does not have to be the end of everything for you. We have all done something like that. It does not have to be a downward decline. You can just come back. You can come and confess it and clear the sin out of your life. God does not write us off when we sin, but you do need to take steps to seek cleansing and restoration.

Peter asked Jesus how many times one should forgive an offender (Matthew 18:21). Should it be seven times? *'Seven times?' said Jesus. 'No, seventy times seven – and even more.'* But if God requires that of us then we can know that he is like that himself. Saul could have got back to God.

> There's a way back to God
> From the dark paths of sin.
> There's a door that is open
> And you may go in.
> At Calvary's cross is where you begin
> When you come as a sinner to Jesus!

You will never outgrow that! Saul could have come back to cleansing and restoration. His tragedy was that he did not. And since he would not rise up he sank down. Let God cleanse you by the blood of Jesus. He will redeem the situation, forgive the mistakes and pick up with you once again.

Chapter 15

Striking a Blow for Freedom
(1 Samuel 13:15b–14:15)

After Saul's sin, he continues with the battle. He numbers the people (13:15b). The two armies are near each other at Geba and Michmash (15:16) and the Philistines divide into three companies ready to attack the Israelites (13:17–18). It is one of the low points of Israel's history. Yet in this story we come to a great victory. The people are released from defeat and slavery. At the beginning of the picture the people are in an awful position. They are gripped with fear and timidity. But Jonathan is a hero of faith and totally swings the position around. In the previous chapter Saul had been worried by his diminishing numbers. Now victory is secured by two men acting with boldness and faith.

So often God's people fall into bondage. There is a bondage that arises from timidity and fear of the world. Jonathan cannot bear the thought of the people of God being in continual defeat. He strikes a blow for freedom.

1. **The turning of the situation comes at the darkest hour**. The Israelites are under domination by the Philistines, who have sophisticated weapons. Apart from Saul and Jonathan the Israelites have nothing but farming equipment (13:19–22). So the scene is ominous as the Philistines move towards engagement with the Israelites (13:23). God can release us from bondage in one step. It often happens that way. God will step in and bring deliverance from the thing that holds us in subjection. It may be a damaging habit, a ruinous

friendship. God can set you free in one step! Israel was utterly humiliated but deliverance was not far away. In one single event, Jonathan breaks the bondage of the people.

2. **He used one man**. One day Jonathan makes a suggestion to his armour-bearer. It was unusual and daring. The army of Israel were too scared to put their noses outside the camp in case the Philistines were there. God likes to use bold, daring, individuals. You – as an individual – can be so free, so liberated. Most Christians have no idea of how free and liberated we are meant to be in God's world. We are meant to be free from sin, free from the world, free from the devil. If the Son shall make you free, you shall be free indeed.

3. **Jonathan's faith took the form of instinct**. Sometimes we have a feeling that we ought to do something although we have no special guidance. Jonathan had no special instructions. God had not said to him 'Go to the camp...' It was just a feeling that something ought to be done. He moves tentatively, not even telling his father. He suggests that they go and inspect what is happening at the Philistine camp (14:1). Saul and the remains of the decadent priesthood of Eli were not far away (14:2–3). We remember the ghastly predictions concerning Eli's family in 1 Samuel 2:33–36. The recently rebuked king is in the company of the rebuked priesthood of Eli. What hope is there of victory coming from such a quarter? Jonathan's faith will achieve more than the discussions of Saul and his officials.

The two men find a path between two cliffs that brings them to a point overlooking the enemy camp (14:4–5). Jonathan is a man of faith, but his faith takes the form of instinct. He simply believes that the Lord will give them victory, and that numbers are not important. Unlike his father (13:11) Jonathan was not disturbed by the thought of a small number getting victory. He has a total faith in the LORD's ability to deliver Israel regardless of the seeming desperate plight of the Israelites. He says *'Perhaps...'*. He does not know precisely what will happen. Sometimes faith will take the form of a desire, an instinct, a feeling. We think God is calling us to do something but we are not absolutely sure. Often the desires of our heart are the whispers of the Spirit. We must take notice when we have a desire in our heart to do something for God. Very often it is the very thing that God wants us to do. You do not need a visit from an angel. If it is a good thing, and you have a feeling that you should do it, go forward, tentatively, enquiringly.

Jonathan's instinctive faith is strong faith. He believes God will show the way. He is willing to work apart from the expectations of others. The officials of the land are giving up in despair, meeting under a pomegranate tree. Jonathan believes in the power of God. The Philistines are only *'these uncircumcised people'* (14:6). This is the thing that makes Jonathan the man he is. The Philistines are helpless because they do not have the blessing of God upon them, and Jonathan knows it. He sees God as God. Nothing can stop God! There is really only one issue. The only question is whether God will act with us and for us. God can do anything. 'Maybe God will use just me and you,' says Jonathan. This is all that needs to happen for you to make a break for liberty.

4. **God gave encouragements**. Jonathan finds support from his armour-bearer (14:7). He proposes something which will function as a sign to them (14:8–10). God honours them and the Philistines say something which is God's instruction that they should indeed approach the Philistines (14:11–12a). Jonathan knows with an assurance of faith that victory is theirs (14:12b). It was perhaps the narrowness of the path that made it easy for Jonathan to kill twenty Philistines with the scarce sword that he had (13:22; 14:13–14). God sent an earth tremor and the Philistines were soon fleeing in sheer panic (14:15).

Jonathan could well have had a place in the heroes of faith in Hebrews 11 who by faith *'put foreign armies to flight'* (Hebrews 11:34). We too will be able to bring deliverance to ourselves and to the church of Jesus Christ if we follow the instincts of faith.

Chapter 16

A Door Still Open
(1 Samuel 14:16–15:3)

While Jonathan was waging war in the Philistine camp, Saul's watchmen noticed the commotion (14:16). Saul discovers that his son is missing from the camp (14:17). He begins to get the ark, which apparently has been brought from Kiriath-Jearim for use in the war. Perhaps he feels it will help in the battles he is expecting. Ahijah starts to get the ark [1] ready for carrying into battle but Saul soon discovers that the Philistines are not about to attack him and are in evident panic and alarm. The ark is no longer needed (4:18–19). Seeing an obvious opportunity, Saul joins the battle, supporters flock to join in the fray, and a great victory is achieved (14:20–23). The Philistines had been put down by these two men; Jonathan who had an intuition of faith, and a faithful supporter.

Saul does not appear well in this account.

1. **A leader out of touch with God will be confused and indecisive in implementing God's will**. Saul is clearly vacillating and out of touch with what God is doing. He now appears as a man who has lost the guidance of God.

2. **A leader out of touch with God has to resort to artificial methods of gaining authority**. Saul puts his men under an oath in which they are forced to promise not to eat until the day is over and the battle won (14:24). There is abundant provision for hungry men but they cannot make use of it (14:25–26). It is a foolish thing to deprive men of food at a time of intense physical conflict, but it is Saul's way of trying to impose

authority. Actually **it undermines Saul's authority** because when Jonathan, knowing nothing of the oath, is visibly strengthened by eating, it leads to criticism of Saul (14:27–30). The oath is exposed as totally inappropriate and foolish. So hungry are the men that, although they do not help themselves to the honey, when the day is over (at dusk) they break the Mosaic law by eating meat with blood in it. Saul then feels he has to offer a sacrifice for their sin. He is trying to put right a wrong that he had led the troops into in the first place. The whole picture is one of a confused man, who is trying to do right, but is making a worse disorder of it, and then making a bigger mess when trying to put right what was wrong in the first place (14:31–35)! He sees their sin (*'You have acted treacherously ... Do not sin against the Lord'* (14:33, 34)) but sees no mistakes in his own actions.

Then Saul wants to plunder and slaughter the Philistines (14:36); it is the very thing he fails to do with the Amalekites in the next chapter! Ahijah the priest suggests they consult God and they soon discover God is not pleased with what is happening and is expressing his displeasure by refusing to answer their questions (14:36b–37). Further investigation reveals that Jonathan has broken the vow he did not know about (14:38–42).

3. **A leader out of touch with God can be strangely 'religious'**. We shall find again and again that Saul can use very pious language, and can be very strict about religious observance. We have seen that he wants the ark with him, and is concerned about the breaking of ritual regulations. He feels he has to offer a sacrifice to repair the 'sin' of eating meat with blood in it. Now he 'religiously' wants to execute his son (14:43–44)! Only weird sanctimonious legalism leads to such folly – like the Pharisees who while they were engineering the crucifixion of Jesus were frightened of being legally unable to eat the passover (John 18:28)! Fortunately less 'religious' people have more common sense and Saul's soldiers have enough sanity to see that ritual laws sometimes have to be broken (14:45). Saul has changed since the days when he displayed great magnanimity in connection with his enemies

and said *'Not a man shall he put to death .... the* LORD *has accomplished deliverance...'* (11:13). When people are slipping away from fellowship with the Lord they are able to do and say things that in previous days they never would have dreamed of doing. Saul's folly is seen even more when we realise that he was so distracted trying to execute his son, that he lost the chance to pursue the Philistines further (14:46). Yet despite the very great deterioration in Saul, there still was a possibility of his recovery. He was being quite successful. He fought enemies on every side and defeated them (14:47–48). We are told of his family (14:49–51), including Abner whom we shall hear about later. As Samuel had predicted (8:11), Saul was conscripting useful men into his army (14:52). Three indications let us know that God was still working in his life and he still could have pulled back into spiritual recovery.

1. **God is still leaving a doorway open to recovery for anyone he is speaking to**. God was still speaking to Saul via Samuel. *'Today if you hear his voice...,'* is a phrase in Hebrews 3:7. A person is able to be renewed unto repentance while God is able to speak to him. Samuel comes to Saul with a message to him from God. It is a good sign that God has not totally abandoned him.

2. **God is still leaving a doorway to recovery if you still have your anointing**. Samuel can say to Saul, *'Don't you remember how I anointed you, and the Spirit of God came upon you?'* It is still working in you, says Samuel. Now go and deal with the Amalekites...

3. **God is still leaving a doorway to recovery while you are being called to serve God by God himself**. God comes to Saul and says *'Go strike Amalek...'* While God is still sending us out on his business, he has not abandoned us. The doorway to recovery is still open.

Footnote

[1] Some translations have 'ephod' but the Hebrew says 'ark' and should be followed (see R.P. Gordon, *1 and 2 Samuel*, pp. 137–138, 343).

Chapter 17

Saul's Fall

(1 Samuel 15:1–35)

Saul began well. When we first met him he was a spiritual young man, but he began to deteriorate when he fell into unbelief. For a long time he could have sought God's restoration. The fact that God was speaking to him through Samuel (15:1), and that God was still calling him to fulfil his kingship (15:2–3) was a signal that there was still the possibility of restoration.

Now comes a further stage in the fall of Saul, one in which he ruined his life.

1. **He was only partially obedient**. Saul was obedient in attacking the Amalekites (15:4–7) but disobedient in keeping Agag alive (15:8), and in keeping the best of the flocks (15:9). His disobedience was partly a matter of pride. He wanted to display Agag. The victory of Jonathan (1 Samuel 14) had showed Saul in a bad light. Now he would be able to display a prisoner who would demonstrate Saul's prowess in war rather than Jonathan's. It was also a matter of profit. The animals were valuable.

2. **He ignored warnings**. God tells Samuel the way he feels about Saul (15:10–11), and Samuel prays all night for Saul. This is an indication that even at this stage there is still the possibility that Saul might be restored. Then Samuel goes to Saul with one last word from the Lord. If he responds to a word from God Saul can still be restored. But Saul is elsewhere building a monument for himself (15:12)! Saul is totally blind to what he has done. As always he greets Samuel

with pious language (15:13) and is blind to his partial obedience (15:13). Saul had been told to exterminate everything but while the bleating of the sheep and the lowing of the cattle can be heard not far away (15:14), Saul is claiming obedience to God's command. Again (as in 13:11), he puts the blame on others but admits no fault in himself (15:15).

3. **He hardens his heart towards God's voice**. Samuel puts to him something to consider which is explicitly a revelation from the Lord (15:16–19). But Saul is still full of excuses (15:20–21). This is his last chance. If he does not obey this last word from God he is finished. But he refuses to accept God's analysis.

So God's judgement falls. God wants obedience more than anything (15:22); he hates rebelliousness (15:23). Now Saul is rejected from being king. This is an *'oath of God's wrath'* comparable to Numbers 14:20–23, the point after which God will not *'change his mind'*. God changed his mind about Saul being king (15:10–11) but will not change his mind about this particular judgement. Saul confesses his sinfulness and asks forgiveness (15:24–25) but it is too late for him to get his ministry back. Verse 26 again says that God has rejected Saul from being king. Saul might plead for a change in God's decision (15:27–28), but God will not change his mind (15:29).

The difference between 1 Samuel 15:10–11, 35 and 15:29 is striking. Can God change his mind? He changed his mind about Saul being king but will not change his mind about this judgement. It is an oath that makes the difference. As Psalm 110:4 says of another matter, *'The LORD has sworn and will not change his mind . . . .'*

However, it is notable that it does not say *'the LORD has rejected you;'* it says *'the LORD has rejected you **from being king.'***

Like Esau who could find no place to get his inheritance because the death-bed oath of Jacob had been given (Genesis 27), so Saul will now not be able to get God to change his mind. Samuel no longer will be his adviser in the kingship. Samuel shows kindness to him in not disgracing him before the people (15:30), but will never speak to Saul again (15:31) during Samuel's life. Samuel's last deed before Saul is to attend to the very thing Saul neglected; Agag is executed (15:31–33). Then Samuel leaves; God had changed his mind about Saul's kingship but will not change his mind about Saul's abandonment (15:34–35).

All of this is a classic example of what we find in Hebrews 6:4–6. Saul could not be renewed to repentance. He had hardened his heart (see Hebrews 3:7) and neglected his great salvation (see Hebrews 2:3). It does not necessarily mean that God rejected Saul eternally. 1 Samuel 26:21–25 seems to speak of a deeper repentance than before, and 1 Samuel 28:19 suggests that Saul would be with Samuel after his death and would share the same destiny as his godly son Jonathan. Statements about Saul's rejection always relate to his ministry not to the man himself ('*rejected* ... ***from being king***,' 1 Samuel 15:15); ('*the* Lord *has torn* **the kingdom** *out of your hand*,' 1 Samuel 28:17). Because such a rejection involves an oath after which God will not change his mind (15:29), Saul cannot get back to where he was before this word was given. He is like the Israelites who before God's oath could go to Canaan (Numbers 14:8–9), but after God's oath (Numbers 14:20–24) could not be renewed back to the position where they were before and could not thereafter get to Canaan despite their attempts (Numbers 44:40–45). If afterward he wished to exercise the kingship with God's anointing, he would find no place for a change of heart in God though he might seek it with tears (see Hebrews 12:17). None of this has anything to do with salvation. Israel though rejected **from Canaan** by God's oath was nevertheless forgiven (Numbers 14:20). So was Saul. But his ministry was lost for ever, and with it his eternal reward. We may believe he was saved through fire (1 Corinthians 3:15) and could have been used in other ways but as God's anointed king he was finished.

May we know God has not taken such an oath against us. If we can hear his voice, if we are not dull of hearing (Hebrews 3:7, 5:14), all is well. We can be renewed unto repentance. But we must keep our hearts tender, for a ministry can be lost. And so can an eternal reward.

Chapter 18

God's Mysterious Choices
(1 Samuel 16:1–13)

When we consider the heroes of the Bible, they turn out to be weak people just like ourselves. They are what they are because of God himself!

1. **God has a habit of rescuing us when everything we think we have lived for has collapsed**. Samuel was depressed. His life's work had been to find a king for Israel, but his life's work had gone wrong. Samuel is elderly. What hope does he have of seeing the king who will lead Israel into righteousness and victory over the Philistines?

We sometimes feel that way, but God has a habit of rescuing us. Samuel was told to rouse himself from his depression (*'How long will you mourn...?'*), to prepare himself for achieving his calling (*'Fill your horn with oil'*), to get moving (*'Be on your way'*) and to know that God was leading him still (*'I am sending you to Jesse'*).

2. Then we notice **God likes to secretly prepare his servants**. God says *'I have chosen one of Jesse's sons to be king'* (16:1). God's choices are totally mysterious. We can think of no reason why God should choose us for himself or for his plans. If we are honest we can think of reasons why he should **not** choose us for anything!

At the time we first meet David, he is a true believer, highly gifted but totally unknown. This is quite clear from what happens later in the story. David said later *'The LORD who delivered me from the paw of the lion and the paw of the bear will deliver me from the hand of this Philistine'* (1 Samuel 17:37). It is quite clear that he knows God long before he ever appeared on the scene as the one anointed by Samuel. Most Christians will never be famous internationally. Yet we all like to be 'famous' in our own way. We like to be appreciated. We like to have our gifts recognised. We like to be known for doing at least some things well. Yet every servant of God has to have a time when he is totally unknown, totally unappreciated, when he is living for God alone. So it was with David. It is in days when we are totally unappreciated and living for God alone that God prepares us for great things. David was trained by lonely living, by obscurity, by learning lessons of faith from lions and bears in the Judean wilderness, to depend on God. When David became a famous psalm-writer and soldier it was because of what had been happening to him **before** the time he was called as king.

Samuel arrives in Bethlehem. The elders of the town are nervous (16:4). Did they have a guilty conscience about something? *'The wicked person flees when no one is pursuing'* (Proverbs 28:1)! But Samuel reassures them (16:5). He wants to hold a public meeting and offer an animal in sacrifice. Jesse is evidently a well-known figure in the town. He and his sons are asked to help in the meeting that is about to take place. They are 'consecrated' for the job, probably by ritual washing (see Exodus 19:10; Numbers 8:21). We notice that David is not included. He is too young and has been given the menial task of looking after the sheep that the family own. But though unappreciated even by his closest family, God already has him in mind for himself.

3. **God chooses the despised, the unrecognised**. Samuel thought he knew who God's choice was (16:6), but he was wrong. Samuel looked at appearance only. God was concerned about appearance as well (note 9:2 and 16:12) but the heart had to be taken into consideration also, and that is beyond the ability of Samuel. He needed – and he got – God's special guidance. Seven sons were presented for consideration. But the one God had in mind was the one no-one

thought worthy of even mentioning! (16:7–10). Jesse actually had eight sons (16:10; compare 17:12). Samuel was puzzled. *'Are these all the sons you have?'* (16:11). *'Oh yes, I almost forgot!'* says Jesse. *'There is the youngest'* – he does not bother even to give him a name – *'but you won't want him. We have sent him out in the bush to look after the sheep. He is too young for anything you might want him for.'* But he was the one God wanted! Samuel holds up the whole meeting, maybe for an hour or so, until David was brought to town. David was God's choice. No-one would have thought of it in advance yet one can see wisdom in it. David was obviously fit and healthy (16:12). God's king would have to deal with the Philistines and be a mighty soldier. God's choice was perfect.

If we know Jesus we can know God has chosen us! I suppose we will never be as famous as David but every Christian has been chosen for something. We are *'chosen to be conformed to the likeness of his Son'* (Romans 8:29), and created for good works which God has prepared in advance for us to do (see Ephesians 2:10). The Spirit is ready to give the enabling for whatever God has for us. David was anointed with oil, and from that day the Spirit came down upon David. It was not the Spirit giving him faith. He had faith already, long before this time. The Spirit was giving him gifts and enabling for the work of kingship. God's work cannot be done without God's Holy Spirit. Even Jesus the Son of God needed the Holy Spirit, over and above what he was as the Son of God.

No-one took all that much notice of what happened. Samuel moved on and it was soon forgotten. A few weeks later David was being despised by his brothers as much as ever (17:28–29), and went back to the sheep (17:15). But from then on, David was the Lord's anointed. There was more secret training for him. God had a plan for David's life and was bringing him into it. He does the same for us.

Chapter 19

God's Training; God's Call
(1 Samuel 16:14–17:25)

One way to train a future king would be to send him to court and let him observe a king being king! Next he might be introduced to doing the things a king needs to do. So it is in the life of David.

First, there comes into David's life God's inconspicuous training. God has a habit of gently manipulating our lives so that we get real experience in something we are going to do, and then he plunges us into our calling.

Saul had ruined his life. God had withdrawn from him (16:14). Wild moods of anger (17:8) and violence (17:10–11) had begun. His attendants knew he was being tormented by an evil spirit (16:15). They had discovered that music had a soothing effect upon Saul, and so suggested that they should look out for a musician to play the harp for him. They did not mention the need to call upon God for mercy, but just wanted something to *make him feel better* (16:16). Saul agreed (16:17), and – in the providence of God – one of his attendants knew about David. Not many knew him but the one who did thought well of his courage, his fine appearance and his spirituality (16:18). After his anointing by Samuel David had gone back to looking after the sheep. *'Send me your son David, who is with the sheep,'* was the message of Saul (16:19). So David was given a few supplies and was sent to Saul (16:20).

David knew he was to be king, and that he already had God's anointing for the task, but he had to be content to let

God work it out for him. This was stage one of David's training – observing a king at work. God put David alongside Saul
(16:21). What better training could David have? He was
Saul's 'armour-bearer', witnessing everything that Saul was
doing as king, observing every kind of task that arose in
Saul's life. This apprenticeship did not last for a long time but
it lasted long enough. God's training lasts as long as it has to
but no more. *'Allow David to remain in my service,'* said Saul
to Jesse (16:22). David continued his ministry of playing the
harp to Saul (16:23).

It was not only training in kingship, it was also training in
psalm-writing! Later David would become famous for his
psalms which to this day often soothe our spirits when we are
in distress. When and where did David learn to exercise this
ministry? He had learned to play the harp in his solitude while
looking after sheep. He learned more about calming distressed
hearts in the palace of Saul. It was all training for the future.

**Next, there comes dramatic introduction into position as
Saul's second-in-command**. Again we notice how the whole
procedure is utterly of God, utterly without any manipulation on David's part.

David was back with the sheep (see 17:15). Despite his
contacts with the palace David was still *'only a boy'* (17:33),
still despised by his brothers (17:28), still being given small
jobs to do for his father (17:17). The Philistines were gather-
ing their forces ready to totally crush the people of Israel
(17:1).

The scene is a dramatic one. There is a valley between two
hills. The Philistines are gathered on one hill; the Israelites are
on the other hill (17:1–3). The Philistines reckon they have the
ultimate military weapon: Goliath! He is about three metres
tall, heavily armoured and accompanied by his shield-bearer
(17:4–7). He stands in the valley and shouts out his invitation
to settle the war by one-to-one combat. War by combat of
two heroes was not common but with a hero like Goliath no
doubt the Philistines thought it was a good idea! Goliath
mentions Saul, hinting that Saul himself should accept
his offer (17:8), pointing out that it would settle the war

decisively (17:9). He is confident and defiant (17:10) and creates panic both in Saul and in the lower ranks of the army (17:11).

It is in that setting that we are once again introduced to David. We are again told of this family with its eight sons, one of whom was decidedly the junior (17:12–15). We discover how David was present when Goliath was shouting his defiance; he was bellowing his message daily for forty days (17:16). David was sent by Jesse to take supplies to his brothers (17:17) and was specially told to pay his respects to the commander of the unit (17:18). This means that David would be noticed by someone high in authority, and yet it was not David's manipulation but his father's instruction. He is told by his father to come back afterwards (17:19) and given direction to where the battle was taking place (17:20).

A marvel of God's timing takes place. David arrives at the very point where the armies are moving into position (17:20–21). He gets on with what he was sent to do and goes straight to his brothers (17:22). At that very point Goliath is shouting out his challenges (17:23). David witnesses the fear of the Israelites (17:24) and hears about the great rewards that will come to anyone who could deal with Goliath (17:25). God has prepared him for his next step towards kingship, which will be largely concerned with overcoming the Philistines. So he is naturally, easily, and decisively introduced into his life's work.

We know the rest of the story. David kills Goliath (17:26–54). Saul takes greater notice of David and keeps him with him (17:55–18:2). In no time at all he is the close friend of the king's son (18:3–4), in high office and much respected by everyone (18:5–7). There can be nothing higher except the kingship itself and Saul's jealousy of David begins (18:8–9).

But we are running ahead. Our task as we look at 17:1–25 is to notice God's hand in all of this. It is totally without manipulation on David's part. God himself has brought something into the story of Israel that will take his chosen king from the sheep-fields to the highest position in the land under Saul. David's days with sheep are finished; from this point on David was shepherd of Israel.

Chapter 20

Goliath

(1 Samuel 17:26–54)

Before the incident with Goliath David was generally unknown. Suddenly something happens that introduces him to prominence.

1. **David was interested in reward**. *'What will be done for the man who kills this Philistine?'* he asked (1 Samuel 16:26a). We may ask, are the servants of God to encourage themselves in God by the thought of how much they will get if they serve him? Is this selfish? But what would come to David would be a further opportunity for fulfil what he knew he had been anointed to do. God's rewards for service consist, amongst other things, of further opportunities to serve God. Jesus certainly encouraged us to go for heavenly reward and no-one can be more spiritual than Jesus (see Matthew 5:46; 6:1–18). Actually the theme of reward is all over the Bible. Can it be wrong to want more of God, more opportunity to serve him, more occasions to be pleasing to him? David was interested in the next stage of his calling. Every Christian should be the same.

2. **David saw the same facts as everyone else but viewed them differently**. They all saw the same giant, heard the same thundering threats, yet David viewed them differently. This is what faith is. It is seeing the same facts as everyone else sees but viewing them differently. Everyone else thought Goliath could not possibly lose. David thought Goliath could not possibly win. The people and Saul react with fear. David reacts

with indignation. *'Who is this uncircumcised Philistine...?'* (17:26b). They want to escape (17:24). David wants to go and get rid of this enemy of God. The Christian is a person who sees things differently from everyone else. We look at God's enemies and see they are outside of the help and power of God (*'uncircumcised Philistines'*), that they cannot win because they are defying God, and that anyone defying God is vulnerable to collapse.

3. **David went forward with a mixture of encouragement and discouragement**. He gets the encouragement of knowing what blessings will come if he goes forward in faith (17:27), but he also has discouragement from his own family (17:28) who criticise his purpose (*'Why...?'*), his sense of responsibility (*'With whom did you leave the sheep?'*), his character (*'how conceited you are'*), his innermost motives (*'how wicked your heart'*), and his seriousness (*'you came down only to watch'*). All of this was quite slanderous and he protests (17:29) but does not occupy himself with criticism overmuch (17:30).

4. **David uses spiritual logic**. In the providence of God the interest of David gets to the ears of Saul, and David is summoned (17:31). Saul does not seem to recognise his one-time armour-bearer. Maybe David has added a few years and a beard since they last met. David is confident (17:32); Saul is sceptical (17:33). But then David gives his reasons for confidence. It is spiritual logic. The God who has been with him before will be with him again (17:34–37a). David has known the help of God before. He uses an argument based upon his knowledge of God; it is this that gives him this assurance of faith. *'The LORD who delivered ... will deliver...'* (compare 2 Corinthians 1:10).

5. **David started in faith and continues in faith**. Saul thinks David might be right, and might just possibly win – but only if clothed with the proper equipment! He still has not got the point. David is not trusting in himself, although he expects God to use him. And he is not trusting in powerful weaponry. He is trusting that the gift God has given him and that God has used before, will be used by God again. He goes out to Goliath *'with deep conviction'* (see 1 Thessalonians 1:5) that

God is with him. Here is the fruit of his youthful years of fellowship with God. Saul's carnal thinking tempts him for a few moments (17:38–39a) but he soon realises he must not do things in Saul's way (17:39b). He goes out with his sling, trusting that God will be with him again as he had been with David in his conflicts against the lion and bear. He takes his sling and stone, plus four spare stones (17:40). (I like the idea that he was ready for more champions; we know at least of Sippai, Lahmi, and another unnamed giant descendant of Rapha – see 1 Chronicles 20:5–8.)

6. **His battle is a battle between worldly confidence and faith**. Goliath is confident in his superior strength (17:41), despises David's apparent weakness (17:42), is scornful (17:43a), religiously calls on unnamed gods (17:43b), and is arrogantly assured of victory for no other reason than his self-confident assessment of his superiority (17:44). Where Goliath trusts weapons and strength, David trusts God (17:45). Goliath's gods are unnamed and gives Goliath no fellowship; David's God is named. He is Yahweh, the LORD, the God who has been known to defend his people (17:45). Goliath expects to relish victory; David expects to relish God's name being better known (17:46). Among Israelites and Philistines alike the character of God will get known (17:47) and the method of God's working will be appreciated (*'not by sword or spear'*). David's faith and assurance is fulfilled. Goliath is knocked unconscious, and killed with his own sword. The Philistines are routed. Trophies of the war are carried off and eventually come to be housed in Jerusalem (which was not yet in Israelite hands), in David's tent.

The entire incident was a demonstration that David was what Israel needed, a hero of faith, a man who knew God. David has taken another step towards becoming king.

David also prefigures Jesus. We see Jesus in his people both before he came and after he came, and in David more than any other. Sin and Satan held us in bondage; Jesus was our conquering hero who slew our great enemy by his faith. As the Israelites rallied to faith because of the faith of David (17:52), so we *'live by the faith of Christ'* (Galatians 2:20).

And then we too can be 'kings' in Christ, slaughtering our Goliaths because we know our God and look at his enemies with the eye of faith.

Chapter 21

Fame – Friend – Foe

(1 Samuel 17:55–18:30)

If we are to be used by God we will have to face differing opinions of us, close relationship with others, and enmity: fame, friends and foes.

David has been anointed by the Spirit, has received some initial training in Saul's service, and now becomes a national hero.

Several things happen to him as a result of the slaying of Goliath.

1. **Fame**. Suddenly David becomes well-known. It happens as soon as he starts walking out to meet Goliath. Saul, who had shown no interest in David's family background before and did not recognize his former armour-bearer, now wants to know all about him (17:55–58). The people were expecting he would offer the conqueror the privilege of marrying into the royal family (17:25). Not surprisingly, Saul wants to know about David's place among the families of Israel (17:56). David is rising into prominence. Before, the question was whether he would be able to handle obscurity. He was anointed the king by Samuel and by the Spirit. But he had to live in obscurity, with scarcely anyone knowing that he had received such a high privilege. But now he has the opposite situation to handle. As a result of the Goliath incident he will be abruptly pushed into national prominence and will be living with the king himself. David has to be like Paul who said he knew how to be abased and how to abound,

and could face any and every circumstance (Philippians 4:11–12). David has had to cope with humiliating circumstances. Now he must cope with exaltation and success. David had been discounted by his father and despised by his brothers. But he had lived for God! The question now is: as he moves from obscurity to fame, will he still be able to cope? Will he once again learn to live on God alone? Will he learn neither to be depressed by obscurity or elated by fame? The psalms that David wrote give us the answer. He learned to look to God alone.

2. **Friendship**. God was with David, and gave him what he needed at this time, a close friend. He and Jonathan became close in the Lord and David had someone who knew about the life of the palace and could be an advisor and counsellor to him.

How did this friendship begin? It had a spiritual base. Saul took David back to the royal house and started talking with him. David no doubt told Saul more about the spiritual experiences that were the background to his killing Goliath. Saul probably was not impressed, but Jonathan was (18:1). The fact that David and Jonathan were in the same house enabled the friendship to grow (18:2). It was **covenant-friendship**; they swore oaths of loyalty to each other promising that nothing would separate them (18:3). It was **generous friendship**. Jonathan could see that David would need some garments appropriate to his new situation as military-commander staying in Saul's house. He immediately gave David what he had himself (18:4). It was **friendship free from jealousy**. It was surprising that these two young men became such good friends, because one would expect them to have been fiercely hostile and jealous of each other. Jonathan was expecting to be the next king. Yet David knew and Saul was soon to start guessing (18:8) that David would be the king, not Jonathan. Still, no jealousy ever came between David and Jonathan.

It is similar to the friendship of Jesus. Jesus' friendship is covenant-friendship; he swears never to leave us or forsake us. Jesus covers us with his protective royal clothing – his righteousness and his status as the King's son. He gives us the *'belt of truth'* that holds us firm in the midst of conflict. Jesus gives us a short-distance weapon (the 'sword' – the Word of God) and a long-distance weapon (the 'arrow' of prayer that can be fired over long distances!).

3. **Foe**. David had not only a close friend but a close enemy. He had to face intense jealousy and animosity. Within a short time he was a military commander of high rank and popular with everyone (18:5). When the men went out to war with David leading them, crowds of women met them as they returned from battle, singing songs in praise of David (18:6–7).

If he was tempted to pride he had something to keep him dependent on God. Saul was jealous (18:8–9). David had taken up his previous task of soothing Saul's moodiness (18:10) but now it roused him to intense violence (18:10b–11). Saul tried to remove him from the palace and put him in danger (18:12–16). Then he offered him status in the royal family but on the understanding that he walked into increasing danger to his life (18:18). David's humility and Saul's instability combine and the idea is abandoned (18:19–20).

Then the opportunity comes again for Saul when Michal falls in love with the young national hero. Saul is delighted and without putting the idea to David face-to-face sees that he gets to hear he must walk into even greater danger (18:21–27). Great exploits have to be performed within a time-limit (18:21, 26). Saul feels sure that somewhere along the line David will be killed.

How does one live with such enmity? God gives the protection (18:28). David had to learn how to stay cool under the ever-present schemes of a cunning enemy. It has often been that way with the people of God, and it was the experience of Jesus. But it is all part of our training. We have to learn to live on God alone. David grew in favour with God and in favour with Saul's own daughter (18:29). Even greater fame came to him (18:30). His training was continuing. God was taking him steadily towards the kingship and using him along the way.

God has a calling for all of his people. He will train us for it, in ways no humanly devised programme could ever do. When he is ready he will bring us into our finest hour. Meanwhile we serve him along the way and one step trains us for the next step.

Chapter 22

When Troubles Intensify
(1 Samuel 19:1–20:42)

Saul's hostility continues (19:1) but everyone around him feels differently. Saul's bitterness results from his not being able to be renewed to repentance.

David must have felt that he had had more than enough troubles and testings. But sometimes God puts us through one level of trouble only as the first stage to putting us through something more intense than we ever thought we would be put through. The hostility towards David was to reach heights that he never dreamed he would face at that time when Samuel was pouring oil over his head and telling him he would be king. Jeremiah put it like this: *'If you have raced with men on foot, and they have wearied you, how will you compete with horses?'* (Jeremiah 12:5).

So David is now plunged into intense and bitter hostility from Saul and has to live that way for several years. When God has plans to use us he will train us accordingly. If his plan for us requires immense ability to withstand troubles, he will toughen us to one degree after another until we are able to survive even amidst intense troubles. It happened to Jesus. He *'learned obedience through the things he suffered'* (Hebrews 5:8). This does not mean that Jesus was ever disobedient, but the Father put ever-increasing pressure upon him.

God taught David that he is able to sustain us amidst the greatest trials. (1) **He can give us friends and supporters who will help sustain us**. Jonathan's attachment to David is strong and he is a good friend to David in trouble. He reveals the way things are (19:2), passes on more information from his father (19:3), intercedes for him (19:4–5), gets his father to take an oath concerning the safety of David (19:6) and restores him to the father's presence (19:7). The resemblances between Jonathan and Jesus are noticeable. When we are in trouble, there may be someone who is like Jesus towards us, favouring us and helping us.

Michal, David's wife, is also a sympathiser. On another occasion when David has been successful in war (19:8) and God hands Saul over to a spirit of jealousy (19:9), David narrowly escapes with his life (19:10). Saul wants to kill him, but without any publicity since David is a popular figure (19:11). Michal helps David escape (19:12–13), and takes evasive action to give David time to get well away (19:14–16), pretending that she had no choice in the matter (19:17), but slandering David in the process.

So a new phase in David's life begins. It must have been hard for him. With everything that happened before; his anointing by Samuel, his rise to fame and popularity, how had it had come to this, that he was now nothing but a fugitive? He escapes to Ramah where the elderly Samuel is in retirement. The two of them go to Naioth (19:18).

God not only gives friends; (2) **He can give miraculous deliverances**. Saul hears about David's stay with Samuel (19:19), and sends soldiers to take David (19:20). But they are overwhelmed by the Spirit and *'prophesy'*. (The word *'prophesy'* in Samuel often means *'fall into incoherent ecstasy.'*) What happens to the soldiers makes it impossible for them to arrest David. It happens three times (19:21–21) and then to Saul himself (19:22–24). When the attacks are intensified the help from God is intensified also.

After a while even these supports and encouragements are taken away from David. David is now forced into a higher stage of trouble and tribulation. It comes about in a way that makes it quite clear that David is not running from trouble. That would not have done him any good. We have to stay where we are until God makes it quite clear that we are to move elsewhere. David's new life is forced upon him. David and Jonathan hold a conference. David runs only after consultation with a wise friend. Jonathan is a *'brother born for adversity'* (Proverbs 17:17). David places his case before Jonathan and takes counsel. The question is: is there any chance of David ever being able to come back to the palace? A way is devised to find out (20:1–23). David misses a royal dinner, and through Jonathan will discover Saul's reaction. But the news is bad. Saul is worse than ever (20:24–34). David and Jonathan meet in secret as arranged and reluctantly say their farewells to each other. They will never live together in the palace again (20:35–42). Jonathan has been a good friend, loyal, practical, self-effacing. But they have to part and David *'suffers the loss of all things.'* He takes one step further down the dark road of sufferings. Almost everything is taken from him. He has no family life, no friends close at hand. His reputation is shattered under the slander of Saul. His youthful romance with Michal is finished, for she is not in touch with him. Her last words were words of slander (1 Samuel 19:17b).

Anyone much used by God is likely to have to *'suffer the loss of all things.'* Even close friends and family might be taken away in one way or another. It was not that David **voluntarily** gave up these things that might sustain him. They were **taken** from him.

What David is learning is (3) that **God stays with us through deprivation, weakness and failure**. For the next few chapters of the story, David is not at his best. Not only does he suffer the loss of all things, he himself does not respond well to the deprivation. We can sympathize. Who could stand up to such viciousness and injustice? David shows signs of panic and self-concern, energetically pleading his innocence, loudly bemoaning his danger (20:3), developing a foolish piece of offended righteousness (20:8b). But no self-pity has any effect on God. God has some tougher training still, but God will stay with him despite everything. It looked as if the kingship was lost for ever. But it was on its way, and David was still undergoing training for his life's work.

Chapter 23

Desperate Days
(1 Samuel 21:1–22:1)

God allowed David to go through a lengthy period of agonizing trouble. Anyone who is going to be used by God can expect difficult days before he gets to the time when God uses him. The very troubles are part of our training. Sometimes we make many mistakes. But God *'overrules for good'* (Romans 8:28) and eventually even our mistakes train us also.

At the stage of his life we are considering, David is going through a bad patch. He has run away. It is difficult to know whether he should have done that. Some commentators are highly critical of him. I know one thing. I would have done the same as David. I would have run for my life! But while David is running he often does things that are awful. We must sympathize with him. He has spent nights out in the open air. He is tired. He has no food. He is intensely anxious.

He arrives at a place called Nob, where Ahimelech the high priest lives. There is a sanctuary there. Immediately Ahimelech wants to know why David and his men (*'those with him'*) (Luke 6:3) have come to Nob, unaccompanied by any army to attack the Philistines (21:1). The truth is that David has suffered the loss of all things. But he does not want to admit it. David lies (21:2) and asks for food (21:3). The only food available is the bread that was used inside the sanctuary at Nob (21:4–6). The men eat it. Strictly speaking it was illegal! But Jesus used this very story to make a point about the Mosaic law. The Mosaic law can be divided into levels of importance, and it is a basic principle with Jesus that laws about compassion and human need are more important than laws about ritual and ceremony. The rules about not eating the 'holy bread' were just ceremonial regulations. When men are starving, laws about compassion are more important. The rules about ritual may be broken without fear.

Then he lies again. The priest asks whether his men are ceremonially pure. 'Oh yes!', says David. *'My men always keep themselves ritually pure when we are on this holy work of defeating the Philistines.'* He is lying. He is not on a secret mission from Saul. His few companions are not looking for Philistines but running from Saul. But he will say anything to get some food! We must not be too hard on him. When Jesus referred to this time in David's life he did not have a word of criticism and spoke only of David's hunger (Mark 2:25) and his concern for his men (Mark 2:26b). He said not one word about any sin and only spoke of compassion!

While David is at Nob there is someone watching all that is going on. Doeg, a supporter of Saul, was watching (21:7). It would have tragic consequences.

Then David tells more lies to persuade Ahimelech to give him a sword (21:8–9). *'The king was so important and I was in such a hurry I had to leave my sword behind.'* There was no king's business. It is strange that David accepts Goliath's sword. It had not done Goliath any good! And David himself was the one who said *'You come to me with a sword . . . but I come to you in the name of the Lord . . . '* (1 Samuel 17:45). But now he is so distressed and half-crazed with panic he is in effect saying to Saul 'I am not coming to you in the name of the Lord; I am coming to you with a sword . . . '.

In desperation he goes to Gath, one of the Philistine towns. Saul will certainly not want to come there! But he is immediately recognized and can think of nothing better than to feign madness so as not to be treated as a dangerous enemy of the Philistines (21:10–15).

So he had to keep moving. He is reduced to an even lower expedient. There were many limestone caves in the region where he was seeking to escape Saul. The caves made good hiding places, and in one of them David found a place adequate to be a refuge and a temporary home (22:1).

Why should David be put through such a time where he is at his wits' end, where he is pressurised into lies, where he acts in a way that brings scorn and disgrace upon himself? He had been promised a palace but all he has is a cave.

1. **It would produce sympathy in David**. It is easy to criticize others when one's life has been cushy and easy. But David would never be able to forget that he had had his patience and endurance tested to the limit.

2. **It would teach David about grace**. David would never forget that when he was full of sin and impatience, when he was lying to Ahimlech and disgracing himself before the enemies of God, that God did not abandon him. We have all known times when we have done things where, if God had entirely written us off, we would have not been in a position to complain. But God does not deal with us as our sins deserve. David would be more tender in dealing with people, after he had himself been dealt with so tenderly by God.

3. **It would teach David about the marvellous deliverances of God**. When David was at his worst and could find no help anywhere, he could only flee into a desert. There is one place there where he is not likely to be found immediately, the cave of Adullam. It was not a palace, but it was enough. When we are at our wits' end, when we have let God down badly, when we are turning to all sorts of desperate expedients to extricate ourselves from our troubles – God is likely to step in and provide a temporary rescue. God will not let us be tested beyond the level of what we can bear (1 Corinthians 10:13).

Chapter 24

Progressing in God

(1 Samuel 22:1–23)

God knows how to give us a break when we are desperate. David was given a short time where things were relatively easier for him. Adullam was not the palace, but it gave David a time to recover. At Nob and at Gath David was at his worst but he has now got back his poise after the terrible days when he felt close to losing his life and had no idea where to run to. He now recovered his sense of responsibility and began to act like a future king.

1. **A future king will take responsibility for the needy**. This is the very essence of what the Bible means by 'kingship'. David begins with his own family. They have joined him (22:1), because they are in danger. Saul is likely to get at him through his family. They had been critical and scornful of him in days gone by (16:11; 17:28), but he does not hold that against them. He is likely to be in danger for a while yet so he must find some place for them to be safe.

2. **A future king must learn to lead a very varied company of people**. The people who joined David were an unplanned army of supporters (22:2). Some were in trouble and debt and no doubt thought it useful to 'disappear'. Some had perhaps suffered under Saul's tyranny. Some were dissidents. Some were good men like the prophet Gad and priest Abiathar. But it was just the kind of mixture that David would have to lead when he became king. What better time to start learning how to be a good leader? Later, David was a brilliant king, soldier

and politician. Where did he get his training? In the cave of Adullam!

So he took care of people, beginning with practical provision for his family (22:3–4). He sends them to Moab. Perhaps he had a good relationship with the Moabites, since his great-grandfather had married a Moabitess (Ruth 4:21–22).

3. **A future king cannot rest for ever**. Soon David has recovered and Gad advised him he must not stay too long at Adullam but must *'go into the land of Judah'* (22:5). A future king cannot be simply waiting around in a cave of Adullam, in the borderlands between Judah and Philistine territory. He must take the initiative. He must be well-informed and well-known among the people of God. Leadership is not passively enjoying a title. It is a matter of aggressively finding out what is happening and doing what needs to be done. *'Go into the land of Judah!'* is the word David needs at this time. He must not remain outside the centre of action. If (as I believe) 'stronghold' refers to the cave itself, it must have been easy to protect. Perhaps (like the caves of Qumran) it was high up on the side of a cliff.

Gad's word is an appeal for a step of faith. To go back into the central land of Judah is to trust in God to keep him in the place where Saul is seeking David.

4. **He must continue to cope with unreasonable hostility**. It is not simply that David has to put up with an incident or two. The hostility he is receiving is self-righteous; Saul thinks God is on his side (see 23:7). It is pompous; we can just imagine Saul holding court under a tamarisk tree, with all his officials around him (22:6). It is vicious; Saul feels quite happy to appeal to greed (*'Will the son of Jesse give ... fields and vineyards?'* 22:7) and to ambition (*'Will he make all of you commanders ... ?'* 22:7). It is scornful; he will not even use David's name (*'the son of Jesse,'* he calls him).

He puts all the blame on others, blaming his servants (*'no-one tells me'*), his son and David himself (22:8). He seems to have forgotten the spear-throwing!

No injustice is harder to face than injustice which is illogical and unreasonable. It is infuriating to have an enemy one cannot reason with! But David has to live with it. If he cannot stay cool under an unreasonable enemy, how will he be able to be king? There will be many who are like Saul that he will have to relate to.

5. **He had to persist in faith amidst complex responsibility**. First he has to cope with guilt-feelings over a tragedy. Doeg had witnessed the help Ahimelech had given David and now sought to ingratiate himself with Saul by telling all he knew (22:9–10). Saul, as vicious as ever, summons the family of Ahimelech, lashes out at them with violent slander (22:11–13), refuses any explanation (22:14–15) and orders the death penalty (22:16). When his servants hinder such obvious cruelty and injustice (22:17), Doeg is willing to do the work (22:18), killing the entire company of eighty-priests and annihilating the population of the town of Nob (22:18–19). Only Abiathar escapes (22:20), reports to David (22:21) who blames himself (22:22) and takes Abiathar into safety among his own men (22:22).

What a stressful life. How bad David must have felt about Nob. If had not been going through such a bad phase of panic and unbelief, the people of Nob would still be alive. It was all a rich and varied experience. In the midst of it all David refuses to let anything move him. He settles into the task of leadership. Soon the four hundred will be six hundred (23:13). His men love him (as is shown by the story of 2 Samuel 23:13–17, coming from the same period of his life). He was trusting in God, as his psalms from this period reveal. Whatever failures he had been through, however much he felt bad (22:22), he persisted in faith. In all these events Saul is deteriorating but David is maturing. In the kingdom of God nothing ever stands still. Saul is moving steadily towards reaping the results of his wickedness. David is growing steadily in spiritual experience of all kinds. Saul is maturing himself for judgement. David is being matured for kingship.

Chapter 25

Learning From Experience
(1 Samuel 23:1–18)

At this point of David's story, he is being brought into new levels of training and preparation for the kingship. He is getting close – although he does not know it – to the days when he will be the king. Five more aspects of his training stand out.

1. **David was given the work of a king before he was given the title of a king**. The major task of the king of Israel at that time was to rid the land of the Philistines. Saul was neglecting that work, but David was given it. He is beginning to function like a king. It is David, not Saul who is told that the Philistines are robbing the village of Keilah (23:1). At such a time it is the work of a king to come to the rescue of his people and defeat their enemies. In the work of God, what counts is not the title we have but the work we are doing. Some have the title but do not do the work. At this point David has the work of a king but does not have the title.

2. **His faith has to steadily increase**. Now David takes on the responsibility for assisting Israel in its conflict with the Philistines. He consults God (23:2) and gets an answer which encourages him to go forward. It requires greater faith than ever, as the comment of his men suggests (23:3). As a good leader he wants to encourage faith in his men also, so when they are doubtful he consults God again. He wants it to be doubly clear that God is with them. God gives confirmation

that the plan has his approval (23:4), and the village is saved (23:5).

3. **He has to be ready to act on principles rather than upon circumstances**. His exploit of rescuing Keilah did not immediately bring anything beneficial to him. He knew what he had done was right. He had consulted with God and had got a clear answer. Abiathar the priest had the 'ephod' (23:6), a lightweight coat of some kind that had stones in it that could be thrown like dice. The way they landed could reveal the will of God. They could say 'yes', 'no' or give no answer. David knew what he did was right yet the results of what happened at Keilah did not seem very useful. It would soon become obvious that the people of Keilah were not eager to have David stay with them; it would bring them into danger.

Here is a good illustration of the dangers of misinterpreting God's providence. God might seem to be acting against David, for his energetic rescue of Keilah brought trouble upon him. God's providence seemed at this time to be working for Saul. Certainly Saul took it that way. He said *'God has delivered him into my hand'* (23:7), and confidently made plans to capture David (23:8). He had not mobilised his army to rescue Keilah, but he was willing to mobilise his army to get David! He feels sure David has walked into a town that could be easily besieged, a place where David could easily be trapped. But the acts of God are easily misinterpreted by someone like Saul who is totally unrepentant. What David has done is right in and of itself. To decide whether it is right by 'interpreting providence' would be a mistake. God's approval or disapproval does not get discovered by our interpreting events without God's word.

4. **David is learning to live by the guidance of God**. He had a resource Saul did not have. He knew God and could talk to God. God was not talking to Saul. David consults the ephod, and God is willing to answer (23:9–12). So David escapes and Saul gives up (23:13). However, Saul learns no lesson from this. He will not *'learn God's ways'* (Hebrews 3:10).

For David these were days of learning how to live on God, and learn from experience. One can see how he had profited from the incident at Nob. Once before a city had been destroyed because of its identification with David. Now David's concern was that the same thing should not happen again. His question was, will Saul *'destroy the city because of me?'* (23:10). A good leader incorporates the wisdom learned from experience into his thinking.

5. **David is learning to rise above ingratitude and live on the provisions of God**. No leader should ever live for the approval of people, because they can cry *'Hosanna'* one moment and *'Crucify him'* the next. David cannot depend on people's gratitude. The people of Keilah gave him no recognition for what he did for them, and are willing to hand him over to Saul.

Yet life is not all betrayal, and God knows how to give us help when we need it. David was being daily hounded (23:14), and must have been asking 'Will this life of being daily hunted by Saul ever come to an end? Will I never see the fulfilment of God's promise that I will be the king?' On one occasion Saul is near (23:15) but the one who arrives is not Saul but Jonathan (23:16–18)! Who better to assure David that he will one day be the king, than Jonathan? God knows how much we can bear and knows when to send help *'in the time of need'* (Hebrews 4:16).

In all of this we are reminded of the *'Son of David'* our Lord Jesus Christ. He too *'learned obedience through the things he suffered,'* and had enemies that watched his every move and wanted nothing other than to see him crucified. He too knew what it was to live on the daily rescuings of his heavenly Father. He too lived above the distractions of ingratitude and betrayal. It was the experience of David that would make him a sympathetic king. And it was the human experience of our Lord Jesus that makes him still a sympathetic King ever living to make intercession for us and send us help from the heavenly throne.

Chapter 26

Finding Encouragement in God

(1 Samuel 23:16–18)

God knows how to send help at the very point where we need it desperately. At precisely the right time God sends a precious friend to help David. The help takes the form of pointing to God. Jonathan encourages David *'through the LORD.'* The ministry of encouragement consists of knowing how to direct a person's attention to God and his promises. Jonathan's encouragement is true and strong. There are five aspects to it, all of which point us to Jesus.

1. **There is an appeal to be free from fear**. Jonathan says *'Do not be afraid . . . '* (23:17).

Again Jonathan is unconsciously being like Jesus, who was yet to come in the flesh. How often Jesus loved to say 'Do not be afraid!' The fact is, God never wants us to be fearful of anything except the possibility of losing his fellowship. The fear of the LORD is the fear of losing God's fellowship and experiencing God's chastening. But no other fear is ever to be permitted in the life of a Christian. God says to us *'Let the LORD of hosts be your fear'* (see Isaiah 8:13) and then you will not need to fear anything else (see Isaiah 8:12). Jonathan knew something of this. He knew that David was likely to be tempted to be afraid. The future looked bleak. His circumstances were painful. David had made big mistakes. Jonathan knew that fear might almost extinguish David's faith. But he knows it also works the other way round, and so urges David to let faith cast out fear.

2. **There is an assurance of continual rescue**. Jonathan says *'Surely the hand of my father Saul shall not find you.'* David has been rescued from Saul before. He needs to know that what he has experienced so far is going to continue all the time. God will go on rescuing him. He can just accept the fact and relax in the confidence that God will always be there when Saul is at hand with his threats.

Often we experience God's miraculous preservations but somehow think we have been rescued 'just this once!' But we need to know that God's rescues will continue. Paul was once *'unbearably crushed'* (2 Corinthians 1:8) and then was delivered (2 Corinthians 1:10). But the deliverance was intended so that Paul might set his hope on the fact that *'He who rescued us . . . will continue to rescue us'* and that he might know *'that he will rescue us yet again.'* God's deliverances are not one-off incidents but life-long faithfulness. David must learn to believe it and find ease and continual refreshment in the truth of it. Saul will never succeed.

3. **There is an assurance concerning the future**. Jonathan says *'you shall be king over Israel, and I shall be second to you.'* One conflict we often have in the life of faith concerns dark forebodings concerning the future. But David has a good future both in general (God will be with him) and in particular (God's precise plans will come about). Any doubts that he might have concerning Jonathan also are answered (*'I shall be second to you'*) which assures David that Jonathan is making no claims upon the throne but also that he will have Jonathan's active support. Jonathan's prediction was mistaken; he did not survive the battle in which Saul was killed. But he knew enough to give David the assurance he needed.

God wants us to feel totally safe concerning the future. Nothing will happen to us that is not within his control. But God does not only assure us in general. From time to time he is able to assure us about particular details. It gives great liberty and freedom when we have this kind of knowledge. He is able to give it still.

4. **There is an assurance that his enemy already knows his defeat**. Jonathan says *'my father Saul also knows that this is so.'*

Despite all of his persistent opposition to David, Saul knew his defeat, and others knew that he knew! But opposition to God's kingdom is never reasonable. Hatred kept Saul going even when he knew there was no hope of success. His hope that God was on his side was pure wishful thinking. Like the devil, Saul *'knew his time was short'*. The very violence of Saul was *'kicking against the goads'* – like another Saul many years later. Jonathan wants David to see that total victory is virtually a present possession. Nothing more is needed than to steadily persist in faith, remain watchful, and watch as God's victory inevitably and irresistibly takes effect. The Christian is in precisely this situation. Jesus is already king of kings. Soon every knee will bow and every tongue confess that he is Lord. By faith we know it now. In his heart the enemy knows it already. *'The God of peace will crush Satan under your feet shortly'* (Romans 16:20).

5. **There is an assurance of covenant friendship**. We read *'Then the two of them made a covenant before the LORD'* (23:18). A covenant was a promise made more secure by the taking of an oath. Jonathan is like Jesus to David. He swears never to leave him or forsake him. He has nothing but goodwill towards him.

Jonathan was like Jesus in another way. His friendship to David cost him a great deal. For David he laid down his throne. Eventually in the midst of doing God's will he laid down his life and David ruled as a result.

Jesus our heavenly Jonathan also left aside his royal majesty and was willing to lose everything that we might be kings and priests to God. He too literally laid down his life that we might reign. Yet unlike Jonathan he goes on ministering Jonathan's encouragements to us, ever reminding us we need not fear, we shall be always finally rescued, the future is secure, the devil is defeated, and Jesus is keeping his oath that he will never forsake us. This is encouragement indeed!

Chapter 27

Learning Mercy

(1 Samuel 23:19–24:22)

Leaders are inclined to be aggressive, pushy people. They would not be leaders if they were not made that way. James and John were ambitious by nature. Paul had burning natural zeal long before he came to salvation. Elijah was ambitious by nature and grieved when he was *'no better than his fathers.'* For all of such people, there is need to develop a more gracious and unvindictive spirit. It was precisely this lesson that David had to learn.

First **something happens where David is apparently at the mercy of Saul**. Jonathan had assured David that he would never perish at Saul's hand (23:17). Soon his assurance was dramatically tested. After the ingratitude of the people of Keilah came betrayal by the people of Ziph. Without provocation on David's part they offered to hand him over the Saul (23:19–20). Saul is still deceiving himself with regard to God's approval and gives a religious-sounding comment, *'may you be blessed by the LORD . . . '* (23:21). He gives them further instructions (23:22–23a) and promises that when the trap is thoroughly set he will return (23:23b). The Ziphites go off to carry out his wishes (23:24a) and in due course Saul and his men come after David (23:24b–25). It seems that Jonathan's assurance is misplaced. At one point Saul and David are going round the same mountain (23:26), with Saul and his men only a short distance behind David. Suddenly Saul receives a message which demands his attention elsewhere (23:27). He has to leave (23:28) and David escapes and goes elsewhere (23:29). The story of David's narrow escape was so notable, the mountain was renamed after the incident. It was striking proof that Jonathan's promise will prove true. God will never forsake David. He will be protected from the hand of Saul every time.

Then something happens where Saul is at the mercy of David. The previous events had left some questions open. We know what Saul would have done if he had caught up with David. But the question is: what would David be like if the situation were reversed and he had Saul in his hands and was able to do what he liked with Saul? And how did he feel about the people of Ziph who, without any provocation on David's part had done their best to deliver him over to the cruelties of Saul?

We shall soon get the answer to our questions, because as the story of David moves forward we find the initiative actually moving away from Saul and into the hands of David. Gradually it is not David who is at the mercy of Saul (as in 23:19–28) but Saul who is at the mercy of David.

Saul heard that David was at En Gedi (24:1) and went in pursuit (24:2). He chooses to enter the very cave where David and his men are hiding (24:3). David's men think the opportunity for Saul to be killed has at last come (24:4a). Now the situation is entirely reversed. David can do whatever he wishes with Saul, and his men are urging him to get rid of his enemy once and for ever.

David is tempted by his men to get his revenge on Saul, but he is restrained by the thought that it was God who put Saul on the throne. Saul is *'the Lord's anointed.'* If God put Saul on the throne, it must be God who puts him off the throne. David will not remove his adversary. He will do no more than cut off the corner of Saul's robe (24:4b) and so demonstrate what he could have done. But even this, as he thinks about it further, he comes to regret. Even cutting Saul's robe was more than he should have done (24:5). He immediately repents and takes the opportunity to explain what he had learned (24:6) and to rebuke his men for the way they felt (24:7a).

After Saul had left (24:7b), David calls out to Saul, treats him with respect (24:8), and reveals to him what has happened (24:9–11). He appeals to the LORD to judge his cause (24:12–15). This is the point. What has happened has led David into learning strong and clear lessons about forgiveness, non-vindictiveness and leaving judgement to God. He is learning to do nothing at all about his enemies in any personal way. When later in David's life, after he has become king and we find David being extraordinarily forgiving, we shall know when and where he learned these lessons. (When he was unforgiving – 1 Kings 2 – it was at a time when he was just about to die and his personal feelings were not involved, but it was important to advise his son to uphold the security of the kingdom.)

This incident reveals the power of mercy. For David's restraint has an effect on Saul. He is deeply moved (24:16) and momentarily brought to acknowledge the rightness of David's words (24:17–18). He feels that David's outlook is remarkable. *'Who has ever found an enemy and sent the enemy safely away?'* (24:19a). Certainly not Saul! For a short time it convinced him that David's genuineness is worthy of reward (24:19b) and that he will indeed be the next king (24:20). Saul actually asks mercy for his own descendants (24:21) and receives a promise to that effect from David (24:22a). For a while it brings to an end Saul's pursuit of David (24:22b) – but Saul's spiritual convictions do not last long.

Learning not to be vindictive is a lesson all Christians have to learn but especially those with the kind of drive that makes them hopeful for leadership in God's kingdom. David is called to be king and is hoping that his kingship will come to him. But *'Mercy, kindness, love ... preserves the king ... his throne is upheld by it'* (Proverbs 20:28). He has to learn to show mercy. It will be something vitally needed throughout his kingship. God has shown much mercy to him. He must live by that same mercy in his relationship even to someone like Saul.

Chapter 28

Lessons in Forgiveness
(1 Samuel 25:1–35)

Perhaps David thought, after his kindly treatment of Saul, that he had learned how to show mercy. But soon something happened that would show him he had not yet got to where God wanted him.

Samuel's death took place at about this time (25:1a). It was a moving occasion, for Israel lost an intercessor and a counsellor. Samuel must have had a reputation for wise advice to the very end. For Saul went to extraordinary lengths to consult him even after Samuel had died (chapter 28)! David was now more alone than ever. He no longer had someone who could teach him lessons about kingship, as had happened before in his life. If he is to be king he is going to have to think for himself and get advice from more than one source. David loses Samuel but he is about to gain Abigail.

Now that Samuel has died Saul might be even more unrestrained. David thought it a good time to move yet again (25:1b). He went to the wilderness of Paran (25:1b), not the distant Paran that we know from elsewhere but another Paran near Carmel and Maon. Alternatively the NIV and Septuagint translations are right in reading 'Maon' not 'Paran'.

The move led to David's coming into contact with a man in Maon, the first character in our story, a man who was in a position to be very helpful to David's men. The man's name was **Nabal**. It means 'fool' and, since it was what he proved to be, perhaps it was the name he was known by after his character developed rather than when he was born. There are examples in the Bible of a name being given to someone after some aspect of his story shows what name is appropriate. He was a wealthy landowner and it was a time for shearing sheep, a time when there was plenty of feasting (25:2).

He had a wife who was intelligent and attractive, but the man himself had an aggressive and unpleasant manner (25:3). It was unexpected in one who was a 'Calebite', that is one who descended from so fine a man as Caleb (25:3), who followed God wholeheartedly (Joshua 14:13–14).

David was in need of food for his men. He hears about the occasion (25:4) and sends some of his men to ask for help. They are to approach Nabal with respect and courtesy (25:5–6), and remind Nabal that his men and David's men have met and have had a good relationship. Although David's men could have forcibly helped themselves to the supplies of Nabal's men, they have treated Nabal's men well and have actually been a protection for them against raiders (*'they were a wall to us,'* 25:16). They are to courteously ask for Nabal's generosity (25:7–8). Such hospitality was recognised in the days of David. To ask for some help was reasonable in the light of the customs of the day.

It is Nabal's ungenerous and aggressive ways that reveal themselves first. He keeps the young men waiting (25:9), and then is deliberately provocative and insulting. David is now famous but Nabal treats him as a nonentity (*'Who is David . . . ?'* 25:10). David is a man of stature but Nabal treats him as nothing more than a runaway slave (25:10), and of unknown origin (25:11).

The second character in the story is **David**. David reveals that he still has more to learn about mercy. Again the issue is willingness or unwillingness to take revenge. David had learned not to touch *'the Lord's anointed.'* But he has to learn not even to want revenge when it is not *'the Lord's anointed'* but a churlish, unpleasant person who deserved no mercy at all and was not anointed for anything! As yet that is

something he has not learned. When David hears what
has happened, he responds with anger and with violence
(25:12–13). There is no mention now of his consulting the
LORD and asking 'Shall I go and attack this Calebite?'
(contrast 23:2).

Any servant of God will have to learn not merely to forgive
the average sinner but an infuriating Nabal. It is one thing to
forgive a king but another thing to stay cool before wilful
provocation and deliberate insult. David had resisted sin
once and refused to kill Saul. But the question is: will we
refuse to yield when the temptation comes again in a more
acute form? David succeeded when tempted to get vengeance
for himself over Saul. But here he fails.

The third character in the story, **Abigail**, is the real heroine.
Abigail shines out as a truly great person. David is taught by
a woman not to take revenge. It is one of the lessons of leadership he needed to learn. Abigail reveals her practicality, her
wisdom and her great skill as a woman of peace. She has a
good reputation, and is known for her approachability. The
young employees of Nabal have witnessed the way Nabal
deliberately insulted David like a bird of prey attacking its
victims (25:14). They know that David's request was reasonable (25:15–16). They also have experienced Abigail's
wisdom and resourcefulness and know that she will know
what to do (25:17). They know it is a waste of time to speak
to Nabal (25:17).

She is worthy of her good reputation because she acts speedily and energetically (25:18). She sees something needs to be
done and acts immediately and decisively. She acts in faith
because she believes something can be done to recover the
situation despite what her husband has done. She decides to
act first and tell her husband afterwards.

She resolves to do what she can to persuade David to relent
(24:18–19). She and David meet (25:20–23) and she puts
her request (25:24–31). David is impressed and grateful
(25:32–35).

Soon David will be king, but God will not let him have the
kingship until he is ready. In these chapters David is learning

advanced lessons of forgiveness. If we are to be used by the Lord, we probably will have to get to an advanced level of graciousness, and God must put us through whatever it takes to bring us to that point.

Chapter 29

Refusing Vindictiveness
(1 Samuel 25:18–44)

Abigail shows great skill in the use of her tongue. Like the rudder of a great ship, the tongue can steer us to where we truly ought to go (see James 3:4). Abigail decides to do what she can to persuade David to relent (24:18–19). Her wisdom is striking. She acts speedily. Disaster could strike at any moment and she is gripped with a sense of urgency. Leaving broken and damaged relationships to some future time would be a mistake. While she is getting the provisions ready (25:18), she lets David know she wants to talk to him (25:19a). She is ready to meet the practical needs of David. His men are lacking food; she takes the supplies they need (25:18). Thus she makes amends for Nabal's rebuff. She shows great skill in her words but words alone will not be enough.

She and David meet at the very point where David is promising himself vengeance upon Nabal (25:20–22). Again we see Abigail's great wisdom and tactfulness. She treats David with great respect (25:23). She has no criticism of him whatsoever and takes all the blame upon herself. David could have been blamed for his vindictive spirit but Abigail has no desire to accuse David of any sin whatsoever (25:24). She acknowledges that her husband was entirely wrong to oppose and disparage God's future king. David was entirely in the right in what had happened. Nabal's reaction was foolish. The Hebrew name means 'fool' and Nabal was living up to his name! If David's men had got to her first, the reception would have been entirely different (25:25).

Then she puts her request (25:24–31). Her reasonings are the arguments of a woman who has faith in God and faith in David as the future king. By her arrival in time God has prevented David from violence (25:26a). She implies that God is the true judge and is capable of dealing with someone as foolish as Nabal. David does not need to take vengeance because vengeance can be left to God (25:26b). She points to the gifts that have been brought, which fulfils David's original request for supplies (25:27). She puts herself entirely in the wrong, asks David's forgiveness (25:28a) and expresses her confidence that God's will for David will be fulfilled without his taking matters into his own hands. His cause is entirely from God (25:28b). It would be better if his kingship did not have any evil in it in as would be the case if David kills Nabal (25:28c). God will keep him safe and overthrow his enemies without David's help (25:29). If David refrains from killing Nabal he will have a good conscience when he becomes king (25:30–31).

David is raised to new heights of forgiveness and graciousness. Abigail's entire plea has assured David that she sees him as God's future king. Everything she says shows a confidence that David will get to his kingdom without the need for bloodshed. It is a plea that generosity and forgiveness will be built into his kingdom in its earliest beginnings. She shows that she believes in God and she believes in David as the future king.

David is impressed and grateful. He immediately sees the truth of what she is saying, thanks God for her and expresses his gratitude to her (25:32–35).

It is another lesson in forgiveness and takes David higher in the life of forgiving graciousness than he had yet known. He now is encouraged to treat all his enemies in this way, trusting God for vindication and refusing to avenge himself. There is reason to think Abigail's influence remained with him the rest of his life. When he later shows great tolerance of Saul's family and the highly offensive Shimei (2 Samuel 16:5–12;

19:16–23), he is standing by the lesson he had learnt from Abigail.[1]

Soon the lesson Abigail taught him is proved and vindicated. Nabal gets to hear what had happened (25:36–38) and is so shocked he dies (25:36–38). Abigail's words about the Lord being able to handle David's cause have been proved correct, as David notices (25:39a).

Immediate blessing and reward come to both David and Abigail. Abigail was a beautiful and intelligent woman, someone fit to be David's queen. She shared his faith, was convinced in God's purpose for his life and had already proved herself to be a spiritually valuable partner for him. David marries Abigail (25:39–44).

There is one thing that spoils the happy ending. David became a polygamist. The spirituality of the people of God had not yet got to the level of the teaching of Jesus and the apostles. Polygamy was tolerated on account of the hardness of the hearts of the men and women of those days. Life in the Holy Spirit outstrips the pre-Christian standards of Old Testament believers. In his youth David had married Saul's daughter. Saul had broken that marriage into pieces. Then David had married Ahinoam. David evidently felt polygamy was open to him as one who expected to be king of Israel. It was following the typical life of a king in the ancient world. If he had exercised patience and not rushed into early and premature marriages, and if there had been no Bathsheba in his life, the story of David and Abigail would have been one of the world's great romances. His learning the lesson of forgiveness was rewarded. But David had already spoiled the story by his impatience and his being too influenced by the pagan view of kingship. Later David's family life was ruined by his polygamy. But the son of Abigail gave him no problems; he had a wise mother.

Footnote

[1] In 1 Kings 2, where David seems unforgiving, he is concerned about the stability of Solomon's new kingdom, not personal vindication.

Chapter 30

Abundant Grace
(1 Samuel 26:1–27:4)

The Ziphites, whom we have met before, once again act the part of spies and betrayers (26:1) and Saul goes off in pursuit of David (26:2). This time David is confident; he starts looking for Saul (26:3–5) and finds him at time when he is unguarded. David wants to go to Saul's camp and offers the opportunity of accompanying him to two men, Ahimelech and Abishai. Abishai volunteers (26:6). He and Joab are David's nephews; Zeruiah was David's sister (1 Chronicles 2:16). They will play a big part in David's life.

David reaches greater heights of generosity to Saul. He and Abishai creep into the camp and find Saul defenceless (26:7). Once again David has the opportunity and the temptation to kill Saul (26:8–11). Sometimes God lets us face an old temptation so that we can know that we have victory over it. David is now far from having any interest in killing Saul. Without harming Saul, he gets proof that he has been in the camp (26:12) and then goes to a place of safety and shouts out his severe denunciation of Abner for not being awake to protect the king (26:13–16). David is actually concerned to protect the king and show him kindness. He is going as far as he possibly can go in showing loyalty and love to Saul.

Paul says if our enemy is hungry we are to feed him. If he is thirsty we must give him drink. David could have added, if our enemy is vulnerable we must take steps to protect him. In such a way we *'heap burning coals'* on the wicked person. This phrase of Paul (taken from Proverbs 25:21, 22) seems to mean that our generosity gives our enemy the possibility of repentance and reconciliation. This is what happened to Saul. David's outstanding kindness towards his enemy works a change in his heart. David insists he is innocent (26:17–18), asks forgiveness if Saul is being used by God to punish him (26:19a), mentions the possibility that others have stirred up Saul against David (26:19b), and expresses his distress at being excluded from his inheritance, the land of Israel (26:19c). He speaks of himself in the humblest of terms (26:20).

David conquers Saul by kindness. David's extreme love and humility has an effect on Saul. For the first time he says 'I have sinned' and seems to be sincere. He acknowledges the effect David's kindness has had on him, and for the first time confesses his folly and wickedness in pursuing him (26:21).

However David does not trust him. He returns the items taken, for he does not wish to be guilty of theft of these small items (26:22). He commends his cause to God's justice (26:23–24). Saul's last words to David are full of repentance and total acknowledgement of the rightness of David's cause (26:25).

It is too late for the kingdom to be restored to him; that has been taken from him without the possibility of restoration. But from this time Saul never again makes any attempt to hunt David. He goes back home and shows no further animosity towards David. His last days were concerned with the Philistines. He will never meet with David again.

David becomes unready for victory. Sometimes the people of God fail to believe God at the very point where they are about to receive an answer to their prayers. Zechariah, father of John the Baptist, prayed for a son but when he was told *'your prayer has been heard'* (Luke 1:13), was not ready for the answer to his prayer. The church prayed for Peter when he was in prison (Acts 12:12) but could not believe Peter had been released as they had prayed (Acts 12:15). Similarly David has now reached the point where he is totally victorious over Saul. Yet he does not see it this way at all. He ignores Saul's invitation (*'Return my son,'* 26:21) and keeps his distance from Saul (26:22), not trusting his professions of repentance. We can sympathize! But actually David would never face any threats from Saul again.

It often happens that when victory is but a step away we collapse and are ready to give up altogether. David is actually at the end of his troubles with Saul, yet is at precisely this point that he falls into bleak despair. *'I shall be destroyed by the hand of Saul'*, he says (27:1). At the very point of victory he does the most foolish thing he ever did in all of his wanderings and evasions of Saul. He joins the Philistines (27:1–3)! It was entirely unnecessary. Saul was told where David was but had given up his enmity towards David (27:4).

Since David did not 'endure to the end' at this point one might think that he would have ruined his calling. Once before David had said *'There is only a step between me and death'* (20:3). Now he is again in dismal despair. But God does not withdraw his plans for us easily. David's fit of despair does not make God give up on him. God has called David to the kingship. When our wobbly faith is anchored to God's great faithfulness our weaknesses do not destroy God's call. David is not persisting in long-term rebellion (as Saul had done). He is simply at the end of his tether and God's faithfulness is not aborted by our fits of despair. *'He does not treat us as our sins deserve....'* David wrote those words himself in Psalm 103:10. God had not treated him as his sins deserved. He had experienced God's forgiving compassion at times when he was at his worst! God can distinguish between a fit of unbelief and long-term rebellion. David was not ready when the kingdom became his, but God gave it to him anyway. God's grace is bigger than we imagine.

Chapter 31

Unbelief Again

(1 Samuel 27:1–28:2)

David is actually at the end of his troubles with Saul, yet he does not know it. He does a foolish thing when he joins the Philistines (27:1). It is entirely unnecessary. Saul had given up his enmity towards David (27:4).

1. **He allowed himself to fall into unbelief**. Despite all that God had done for him and the many times he had been rescued he was saying to himself *'I shall be destroyed by the hand of Saul'* (27:1).

2. **He was leaning on his own understanding**. *'The best thing I can do,'* he reasoned with himself, *'will be to escape to the Philistines'* (27:1). The Christian uses his mind, but the Christian does not trust his mind. It is easy in a time of difficulty to jump prematurely into our own devices. Our own devices can lead us into extraordinary entanglements.

3. **He took others with him into his folly**. His six hundred close allies and their families went with him (27:2–3). It led David into many evils. 1 Samuel 27:4 may be translated *'And it was told Saul that David had fled to Gath, but he did not seek him again any more.'* The extra word in the Hebrew, *'any more,'* suggests not that Saul gave up seeking David because he was at Gath but that Saul would never again be seeking David. David's troubles with Saul were at an end.

4. **David began to live a double life**. He asked for a place to live (27:5). To dwell in the royal city of Gath might suggest that he has secret plans to attack the city. It would also

hinder the secret plans he had to raid Philistine areas. He was given Ziklag (27:6) and for sixteen months spent his time annihilating the pagan tribes that were jointly inhabiting the land alongside the Israelites (27:7–8). On each raid he took the trouble to leave no survivors (27:9a). He would tell Achish that he had been invading Israelite villages (27:9b–10) and made sure no-one was alive that would reveal his deceit (27:11). David's subterfuge led Achish to believe he had completely gone over to the Philistines (27:12).

5. **David's devious scheme led him into attacking Israel**. It was only a matter of time before he would be dragged into something disgracefully identified with the Philistines cause. Soon Achish expected David to take part in an attack upon Israel (28:1–2). Now what would David do?

All of this was disgraceful. True, the Israelites had been told to slaughter the Canaanites and Saul had lost his kingdom for not doing so (1 Samuel 15:2–23). But God's last instruction had been to stay in Judah. Later when David wanted to build the temple, he would be forbidden *'because you have shed much blood upon the earth in my sight'* (1 Chronicles 22:8). David's life was needlessly violent at this point. It would lead him into yet further troubles.

Great crises test our faith. God sometimes lets us fall into acute difficulty so that we are able to see what is the level of our faith. David had been a hero of faith in many great and wonderful ways since his earliest days. Even as a boy he had shown great faith as a shepherd defending his flock against wild animals. The defeat of Goliath had shown great faith in God and had been the beginning of his career as a national leader in Israel. Yet David's faith could still fail him when he was under pressure and God allows him to see it at this time in his life, just before he becomes king. Our faith is faith in God. It is not faith in our own faith!

Great crises test our willingness to seek God. What David failed to do in all of this was to seek God. God had a will and a purpose for David. David could have approached the Lord, seeking his will in this desperate situation he felt himself to be in. But this is where David failed. Later when David's own devices were obviously letting him down badly and he was *'greatly distressed'* (30:6), he turned to God (30:6) and asked the help of Abiathar the priest who had the ephod, the jacket which contained the stones that could be used for finding God's will (30:6). But at this earlier stage in these events David is not living on God.

Hebrews tells us to take care lest in our hearts there springs up an evil heart of unbelief leading us to turn away from the living God. The more resourceful and self-sufficient we are, the more likely we are to turn to our own resources.

It is likely to lead us into entanglements that will be entirely discreditable. David acts as though God is not able to deliver him, despite many deliverances he has been through before, some of them astonishing and dramatic. Had he forgotten the way God aided him against Goliath? Has he forgotten the time he was almost trapped by Saul and God came to his aid in a marvellous way?

It was a good lesson for David to learn at this very late stage in the days before he would be king. If God had not allowed him to stumble in this way he would have gone into the kingship with a self-sufficient attitude. Better to make mistakes like this before he is the king.

David thought Saul was hunting him. Actually there is no problem at all! Saul has given up altogether from his pursuit of David and at the very time (*'In those days,'* 28:1) was moving in a direction that would lead to his final removal (1 Samuel 28).

Our turning to our own devices is always a mistake. The words of Proverbs 3:6 were perhaps written by David's son. *'Trust in the LORD with all your heart and lean not on your own understanding; in all your ways acknowledge him, and he will make your paths straight.'*

Chapter 32

Saved Through Fire

(1 Samuel 28:3-25)

Saul had been rejected from the kingship. He had lost his usefulness, his joy, his experience of hearing God's voice, his ministry as leader of Israel.

If he had accepted the decision of 1 Samuel 15:28–29 and sought to obey God from that point, who knows what blessing might have come to him? Saul could not be renewed to repentance in the sense of getting back to where he was before his rebellion, and before the decision of 1 Samuel 15. As Esau wept and pleaded for his inheritance but could not get back to where he was before Jacob took an oath (Genesis 27:34), so Saul could not get back to where he was before the decision of God. Yet 1 Samuel 15:26 does not say 'The LORD has rejected you'; it says *'The LORD has rejected you from being king.'* What could Saul have done? If at that time he had fallen on his knees before God and had recognised that God was about to raise up a successor, who knows how God might have used him as a colleague of David and Jonathan?

However, following God's decision of 1 Samuel 15 there has only been further wickedness. Saul has lost the possibility of hearing God speak to him **in connection with kingship and conflict with the Philistines**. God might have spoken to him about other matters, but Saul has only revealed more and more his unwillingness to hear God's voice. In despair he tries to get access to Samuel by going to a woman who has given herself over to contact with evil spirits. Saul himself had banished such people from the land (28:3).

The Philistines were about to invade (28:4); Saul is terrified (28:5). God will not answer his attempts to get guidance (28:6). If he had sought thorough forgiveness for his sins he could have re-established some kind of fellowship with God. But God will not give him guidance before he is thoroughly restored and Saul is not taking the pathway of thorough restoration. His ministry is lost for ever. The right thing would have been to call upon David for help.

Instead Saul contacts a medium and visits her in disguise (28:7–8). The woman knows that what she is doing is forbidden in Israel (28:9) but Saul reassures her (28:10) and the séance proceeds (28:11).

Then something dramatic and totally unexpected occurs. God allows Samuel to come back. This was not what normally happened! Delusions and deceptions from evil spirits were all that had taken place before. But on this occasion she sees Samuel, and simultaneously she knows she has been deceived by Saul. The woman cries out in terror. This was not the way her sessions normally went (28:12). Saul questions the woman and knows that the vision is indeed an appearance of Samuel (28:13–14). The text is clear. It does not speak of 'one who had the appearance of Samuel.' It says '*Samuel said to Saul*' (26:15). This is unique and unprecedented in the Bible. The fact that the woman was so shocked is a sign that this was not what usually happened.

1. Samuel confirms that Saul will get no guidance from God concerning his kingship. What is the point, Samuel asks, in this consultation? There is nothing Samuel can say that will help Saul in being the leader of the Israelites against the Philistines (28:16). On this matter Saul will never hear from God and will only face God's enmity as he continues to attempt to be the king of Israel.

2. He confirms that Saul is rejected from being king. It does not necessarily mean that Saul is rejected altogether, but his work of kingship had ended a long time ago and is given to David. Saul's ministry of kingship was finished (28:17–18).

3. He does have a message of mercy as well as judgement. Saul's life is at an end. He will be facing the Philistines the next day. His lifelong rebelliousness will reap its consequence in Israel's defeat. But, Samuel adds, *'you and your sons will be with me'* (28:19). In many ways this is a statement of great mercy. It was mercy that God spoke to Saul at all. It shows that the refusal of God to speak was connected with Saul's ministry having been lost. If Saul had been willing to amend his ways God might have been willing to bless him in other ways. The fact that one thing in our life may be lost beyond recovery does not mean that everything has been lost.

When God speaks it is that we might hear his voice and respond to him in faith. God was speaking to Saul – but his words were not words of guidance concerning the kingship. It was mercy for Saul to be told he and his sons would be with Samuel. They were a believing family. Saul had once been a godly person. Jonathan had shown himself to be a man of great faith. Saul and his sons would be in the unavoidable battle the next day. All of them would lose their lives. Using New Testament language, all of them were about to go to heaven. All of them would be with Samuel. The sure and certain knowledge of imminent death was a call to Saul to fall on his knees and be right with God. Something similar happens today whenever a person has some kind of terminal illness.

Sheer terror follows. It is a mercy to know for a certainty that one is about to go through one's last day. But it is a mercy that is fearful (28:20). His appetite is totally lost (28:21–23a). He eats reluctantly and goes out to face what he knows will be his last day on earth (28:23b).

It was a fearful thing for Saul to fall into the hands of the living God. The Lord was judging one of his people. Saul discovered it is possible to be rejected from ministry after having once had a ministry. He had ruined his life. He would be saved through fire (1 Corinthians 3:15), since there was nothing he had laid up as treasure in heaven.

Chapter 33

Spiritual Restoration

(1 Samuel 29:1–30:10)

We have seen (in 1 Samuel 27:1–28:2) that David did a foolish thing when he joined the Philistines. It was a lapse into un-belief. It was leaning on his own understanding. Soon he was disgracefully identified with an attack upon Israel (28:1–2). Now what would David do?

David was moving steadily towards total entanglement in sin. If he backed out of attacking Israel he was risking his life at the hands of Achish. Yet there was no way he could proceed in the direction of attacking Israel and yet expect to be Israel's king.

Suddenly God intervenes and a surprising turn of events takes place that rescues David. The Philistines get ready to fight Israel (29:1). David and his men assemble with the others (29:2). But this raises questions in the minds of the other generals (29:3a). Achish believes in David's loyalty (29:3b) but the other generals will not hear of fighting alongside David (29:4–5). Achish apologizes but insists David must not be in the battle against the Israelites (29:6–7). It would not be safe for David to seem to be pleased to be released! So he keeps up the pretence and strongly protests (29:8). But Achish is insistent. David must leave immediately (29:9–10).

So David was released from his predicament (29:11). It is a wonderful demonstration of the faithfulness of God. It is not that David had repented of his folly and started calling on God. But even before his repentance God put a limit to the extent that he would allow David to go on in his foolishness.

God is able to keep us from falling (Jude 24). This does not mean that he always will. But he is able to. God allowed David to fall into this folly but to have allowed him to fall even further would have totally ruined David's future as king and this God would not allow. Even without David's repentance God would not allow his servant to ruin his life any further. David had showed much love and trust in God. It was not that he had a totally rebellious spirit, as did Saul. Yet David too could have gone the way of Saul if it were not for the mercy of God.

Then something else happens which brings David to his senses. David has still not come to regret his folly in turning to the Philistines. He goes back to the town that was given him by the Philistines, Ziklag, only to find that the Amalekites had invaded the town, destroying it and kidnapping the women (30:1–3). The entire army was shattered and grief-stricken (30:4). David himself had lost Ahinoam and Abigail (30:5). His army were blaming David and were ready to take violent action (30:6).

It was this that brought David back to God. We have had no reference to David's turning to the Lord since the day he panicked in fear that he would be killed by Saul (1 Samuel 27:1). His fear had been a lapse of faith and his relationship with God had not been a good one since that time. But now *'David strengthened himself in the LORD his God'* (30:6). It means that he turned to God in prayer and cast his burden upon the Lord. He reminded himself of God's mercy and God's faithfulness, and stayed seeking God's face until (like Hannah (1:18)) he found peace and assurance that God had forgiven him and would be with him.

He then turned to seek God's will, by consulting Abiathar and the ephod (30:7–8). It had been some time since he had sought God's will. He did not do this when he was falling into panic because of fear of Saul. Now he wants to trust God's guidance and has ceased to lean on his own understanding.

God is well able to mix our experiences in a way that teaches us what we need to know and puts pressure on us when we need to be brought forcefully back to him. David's experience at this point was needed to drive him back to God. It was also needed as part of his training for the kingship. There would be times after he had become king when he would face disaffection and disillusionment among his people. He would need to know how to regain his authority when facing dispute and disloyalty.

God's working all things together for good is apparent here. David's fainting fit and flight to the Philistines was obviously a low point in David's life of faith. Yet out of it all came experiences that were to be useful to David in later years when he was the king. There are several ingredients in his regaining authority among his supporters.

Firstly, God gave him an assurance that he would be able to regain his lost people and lost goods (30:8). The oracle gave him the assurance that he would recover everything. He goes forward with a sure knowledge of God's will. To move with a knowledge of God's will is a vital part of leadership. Jesus would spend much time in prayer before every major decision so that his actions always were in accordance with a knowledge of his Father's will. David had learned to acknowledge the LORD in all his plans and ventures. God's people are to understand what the will of the LORD is (Ephesians 5:17).

Secondly, David learned wisdom in allocating tasks according to abilities. Some of his men were stronger than others. David made use of those who were capable of sustained conflict, and gave weaker soldiers a task appropriate to their weakness (30:9–10). Some were physically exhausted; David left them at the brook. It was a good use of the varied abilities of his people. He was wisely giving tasks to his men in such a way that he was not overstraining the weak, and was making maximum use of the strong. God's people have gifts that differ (Romans 12:6) and some are weak at points where others are strong (Romans 15:1). We have to *'accept one another, just as Christ also accepted us'* (Romans 15:7).

God's wise ways with David had brought him to recovery and usefulness once again.

Chapter 34

Preserving Unity

(1 Samuel 30:11–31)

God was bringing David back to usefulness in his service. David was not only restored, but he was learning how to keep his forces together as one people. David's kingdom was eventually welded together as a great and mighty empire. Lessons in building and preserving such unity were being learnt at this point before the title of king came to David.

We have seen God give him an assurance he would recover everything, and that David learned how to allocate tasks wisely.

Thirdly, we note that God gave him guidance to speedily find the Amalekites. Sometimes in the work of the LORD one needs the exceptional help of God. God needs to bare his mighty arm and give us something unusual and unexpected. It would seem to be an impossible task to discover which of the various groups of Amalekites that were around were the ones that invaded Ziklag. Then it would be difficult to find their present whereabouts. But this gives God opportunity to display his marvellous ways. When David was in desperate need with his army threatening to rebel, unexpectedly they came across a member of the Amalekite forces. He is someone who has no special allegiance to the Amalekites since he himself is an Egyptian. He is treated kindly by the Israelites and gives them all the information they need (30:11–15). Here was a mark of God's special help in a time of need. When God is giving special help all the factors will come together to make it seem, if not a miracle, at least a marvellous combination of factors. It was wonderful that they should find this young man at all. It was wonderful that he should be an Egyptian with no special patriotism towards the Amalekites. It was wonderful that his having been abandoned by his master would make him all the more inclined to want to help another nation with whom he might have the chance of a fresh start. It is wonderful that he has the information as to the present whereabouts of the people who have abandoned him. When God is giving special help everything will combine to make it obvious that God is with us.

Fourthly, we note that when victory had been given, David is careful to maintain the unity of his supporters. David attacks the Amalekites, defeats them and regains everything that had been taken (30:16–20). Because some of his soldiers had been compelled to fight while others guarded the baggage there was an understandable but divisive feeling that those who had done the fighting should be entitled to the goods that had been recovered. But David would not allow one part of his army to profit from another part of his army. It would lead to jealousy and division and would weaken his army's ability to fight as a united force (30:21–24). It became a permanent ruling for Israel's army and contributed to the unity of Israel's fighting force in later days (30:25).

The same is true of the church of Jesus. Jesus, our heavenly David, takes a lot of trouble to bind his church together, if we could but see it. The various members of the body of Christ, the church, are arranged in such a way *'so that there should be no division in the body'* (1 Corinthians 12:25). The same principle applies even with regard to money. Those who are hard-pressed are relieved by those who have plenty, so that there will be an equality (2 Corinthians 8:14).

How much of the Scriptures are given over to preserving unity among God's people! Not only is it a part of Jesus' intercession (see John 17:21), it is the concern of many of the appeals of the New Testament writings. How often there come appeals to *'stand firm in one spirit'* (Philippians 1:27) and be *'like-minded, having the same love, being one in spirit and purpose'* (Philippians 2:2). Any good leader will see preservation of unity as a skill he must acquire.

Fifthly, we note David took the trouble to secure goodwill among those who might have doubts about him. When he got back to his headquarters at Ziklag he sent some of the goods he had obtained from the Amalekites to the various cities in the areas where David and his men had often travelled in their many escapades. One can see several reasons why David would do this. It expressed gratitude for their support of him. It removed doubts that may have arisen because of his stay with the Philistines. It demonstrated that David's men were sufficiently effective as to have been able to win a major victory with a large amount of booty. A lesser man than David might not have bothered with such careful concern to secure goodwill.

These practical steps that David took to secure the unity of his troops and the goodwill of his acquaintances reveal that David has now become a greatly experienced leader of men. The experience he has gained as a leader of a small army has prepared him for the much larger armies he will have to lead as king of Israel. The unity he has been able to secure among his team of six hundred families prepare him to strive for unity amidst a nation of twelve varied tribes weakened by many years of harassment by the Philistines. David is now highly qualified both in the life of faith and in practical experience of men whether friends or enemies. He is ready for the kingdom. It has taken God many years to bring him from being a shepherd boy to readiness for kingship. God will do the same for us. Whatever our calling he will put us through whatever it takes for us to be ready. If it is a major calling it will take time. God will give us all the attention that we need and give us as much time as it takes for us to be ready. Then God will use us in a way that fits the background we have been given.

Chapter 35

The End of the Backslider

(1 Samuel 31:1–13)

The Philistines' fighting on mount Gilboa is energetic and successful. The Israelites are scattering (31:1) and the Philistines seem to be determined to kill the entire family of Saul. First the sons are killed (31:2). Then Saul is fatally wounded (31:3).

God leaves the backslider on his own. Years previously Saul had *'fallen aside'* (Hebrews 6:6). God had told Saul that he had lost his ministry and was rejected from being king (1 Samuel 15:23). This does not mean that Saul was rejected personally. If he had accepted God's verdict and had allowed God to give the kingdom to his successor, his life might have turned out differently. But Saul persisted in his disobedience. He had lost his ministry of being king in Israel, and it would never be returned to him (1 Samuel 15:29). He lived the remainder of his life without fellowship with God.

At the end of his life it became apparent what it meant for a believer to lose his reward.

1. Saul had already lost his ministry and his anointing as king. He was no longer able to function as king. God would give him no guidance in the kingship.

2. Saul was incapable of being a channel of blessing. Instead he involved others with his own doom. As Samuel had predicted (28:19) the Philistines attack Israel (31:1). The

120

Israelites flee and fall (31:1). Saul's sons fall with him (31:2), as does his armour-bearer (31:5). Verse 6 emphasizes the three groups that fell with Saul: people, sons and armour-bearer.

3. Saul brought defeat upon his people. The lifetime of Saul had been a story of decline for Israel as well as for Saul personally. At one stage Saul had even been more concerned to hunt down David than to hunt down Philistines, which was the reason the people had wanted a king in the first place. Now we reach the end of the story and Saul had led the people into nothing but defeat and deepened subjection to the Philistines.

4. Saul lives to see the reversal of his previous successes. Before he had chased Philistines (14:22); now the Philistines chase him (31:2). Before Philistines had left their bodies along the roadside when defeated by Israel's armies; now it is Israel whose bodies are covering mount Gilboa (31:1).

5. Saul lives without God's special help. The picture is one of his being hard-pressed by the archers (31:3). It is not that he has been hit by them but he is in great distress as he comes under their fire. The psalmist could say *'I called on the LORD in distress'* (Psalm 118:5). But Saul was not in a position to do so. He already knew what the future was to be; Samuel had told him. There was no possibility of God coming to his aid. He knows the Philistines are likely to torture him (31:4), and thinks that to die before they get him would be preferable (31:4). He wants help in committing suicide but can get no help in that (31:4) and so takes his own life (30:5). Like Ahithophel (1 Samuel 17:23) and Zimri (1 Kings 16:18) and Judas (Matthew 27:5) he can see no other remedy (31:4).

6. Saul brings calamity rather than blessing upon those around him. His armour-bearer who could have shared his honour (as happened with Jonathan's armour-bearer, 14:6, 7, 12, 13) instead shares his failure and disgrace (31:5). Three groups of people were dragged down when Saul came to his end (31:6).

7. Saul's fall led to loss of territory. Philistines who before

had been subdued, now came in to take over many Israelite towns (31:7).

8. Saul's fall led to great disgrace. His body was dishonoured by being beheaded. In days gone by it was the Philistine Goliath who had been beheaded (17:51) and his head had been displayed in triumph (17:54). Now that very thing happens to the body of Saul (31:8–10). The news gets sent round the Philistines. His life ends in disgrace (31:1–10) and only the men of Jabesh-Gilead remember him for his past assistance to them (31:11–13).

The way of the backslider gets narrower and narrower. The way of the man of God gets wider and wider. During these years covered by 1 Samuel 16–31 Saul had been in a position of prestige and power as the king of Israel. He was in the highest position of earthly glory that could be obtained in Israel. David's pathway had been rough indeed. He had been despised by his father, apparently. His stay in Saul's palace and his days of glory as the slayer of Goliath had been brief. He had suffered anguish as the object of Saul's jealousy and had *'suffered the loss of all things'*. But now, as the reader knows, Saul having sown to the flesh has from the flesh reaped corruption. David, as the reader of the story can now guess, is moving towards the kingship of Israel and is God's man for the hour. Whose position was the greater, Saul's or David's? The story has made the answer clear. *'The light of the righteous shines brightly, but the lamp of the wicked is snuffed out'* (Proverbs 13:9).

The story will continue (in 2 Samuel) with the account of David. Saul's reputation, despite all his good beginnings, will be a bad one. Our honour comes not through how we started but through how we end. It is he who perseveres to the end that obtains the 'well done' of God and of other people. David endured in the will of God. It is his name, not Saul's, that goes down in history with honour and glory attached to it. Similarly Jesus, our Son of David, *'for the joy that was set before him, endured the cross and despised the shame.'* We have to be like Jesus, David's greater Son, who endured until he had totally achieved God's will for his life. *'Watch yourselves,'* said John, *'so that you do not lose what you have accomplished, but receive a full reward'* (2 John 8). Jesus got to glory. He is able to keep us from falling, so that we hear Jesus himself say to us 'Well done!'.

Appendix

Some Facts About 1 and 2 Samuel

Matters of 'Introduction' do not receive detailed discussion in this book but there are a few basic facts which we ought to know.

The books of 1 and 2 Samuel are actually only one book in the Hebrew original. It was apparently first divided into two books by the Greek translators in the third century BC.

'Samuel' is a book full of stories telling us of the rise of kingship in Israel. This is important to us because much of the Bible is concerned about kingship or kingdom. If you were to put into one word the message of the Bible, what would that word be? It could be 'gospel' – good news. It could be 'salvation'. It could be 'reconciliation'. But probably the best single word that summarises the entire message of the Bible is the word 'kingdom'. It was the word Jesus used to summarise his message. Jesus could have come preaching 'The gospel is at hand', or 'Salvation is at hand'. But the way he chose to put his message was to say *'The kingdom is at hand'*.

Jesus is a king. His powerful work in this world is called 'kingdom'. He makes us to reign and rule with him, so we are kings and priests unto God. His kingdom has come, his kingdom is coming, his kingdom will come. These are the themes of the Bible. It is this that is behind the stories of the books of Samuel and of Kings. They are the story of the rise of God's kingdom in Israel. From them we learn much about God's kingdom as it operates in our times and in our lives.

Five questions will lead us into what we need to know about 1 and 2 Samuel.

Who wrote it? We do not precisely know, but it seems that the book of Deuteronomy kept on being enlarged with historical supplements which were written in the same style as the book of Deuteronomy, which itself comes mainly from the days of Moses. At one point there must have been Deuteronomy-Joshua. Then it got enlarged a bit more and there was Deuteronomy-Joshua-Judges, something like an expanded Deuteronomy, a third edition of Israel's history, all written in the same style. Then there was a 'fourth edition', Deuteronomy-Joshua-Judges-Samuel. Then finally there was Deuteronomy-to-2-Kings, all written in the 'Deuteronomic' style and all building upon the teaching of the book of Deuteronomy.

When was it written? It seems that 1, 2 Samuel as we have it has to be dated after the division of Israel into two kingdoms in about 970 BC (because of 1 Samuel 27:6). So probably Deuteronomy-to-2-Samuel existed as a history of Israel in about 950 BC. The full story Deuteronomy-to-2-Kings was completed later in the sixth century as a kind of 'fifth edition' of Israel's history.

Why was it written? The wise men and prophets of Israel felt it useful to keep a record of the things God had done within Israel's history. So, under the inspiration of the Holy Spirit they felt led to compile this history for the benefit of later ages.

How was it written? The author-editor of Samuel used sources. Some fragments of history had already been written and an author-editor put it all together. Some scholars think they can reconstruct what the sources were. They may be right, but it is hard to prove the scholars are doing anything more than guessing.

How does the story unfold? 'Samuel' – a single book in the Hebrew – gives us story after story concerning how David came to be king. Those who like stories should like 'Samuel'.

It focuses on one person after another. First we meet Hannah and discover how Samuel came to be born (1 Samuel 1:1–2:10), then we read about the events of Shiloh, how Eli's household was faithless and how it was replaced by Samuel's ministry (2:11–4:1a). Then we read about how the ark was lost (1 Samuel 4:1b–7:2) and then twenty years later was recovered (7:3–17). Chapters 8 to 15 deal with the people's demand for a king, their being given Saul, and the eventual failure of Saul through disobedience.

Then the book gets really exciting. We read about David and his early life (16–20) and his life as an outlaw with king Saul hunting for him (21–27). Chapters 28–31 tell us of Saul's final days.

In what we call '2 Samuel' David hears the news of Saul's death (chapter 1) and is made king (chapter 2) but for a few chapters he is still not king of all Israel. There is civil war between David's supporters and followers of Saul (chapters 3–4). Finally David becomes king of all Israel at Hebron, Jerusalem becomes his capital city, he defeats the Philistines and establishes his empire (5:1–9:13). At that point David almost ruins his life. There is a time of war with Ammon (10:1–19). At such a time David commits adultery but is rebuked by God through Nathan, and (although he is forgiven) terrible problems are predicted for his life (11:1–12:31). Chapters 13–19 tell of the immense conflicts he had within his own family and nation. Chapters 21–24 tell of his warriors (chapter 21), his music (chapter 22), his last words (chapter 23) and his self-confidence in numbering the people.

The books of Samuel do not tell of David's death and the handing of the kingdom to Solomon. These come in the early chapters of the books of Kings.

More Advanced Reading

The present work gives a simple exposition of 1 Samuel. More detailed exposition will require some thorough study. The best scholarly commentaries at present on 1, 2 Samuel which I would recommend are *1 and 2 Samuel* by Joyce Baldwin

(Tyndale), *1 & 2 Samuel* by R.P. Gordon (Paternoster) and
'1, 2 Samuel' by R.F. Youngblood (in *The Expositor's Bible
Commentary*, vol. 3, Zondervan). H.F. Vos' *1, 2 Samuel*
(Zondervan) is good and slightly simpler; G.J. Keddie's
Dawn of a Kingdom (Evangelical Press) is good for those who
speak English as a foreign language. For more thorough
exposition of the **message** preachers will still find Matthew
Henry's old commentary useful. I have found helpful W.G.
Blaikie's, *The First Book of Samuel* (reprinted by Klock &
Klock). Tom Houston's *King David* (Marc Europe) is insight-
ful, as is F. Catherwood's recent *David* (IVP). A.W. Pink's
Life of David (Zondervan) is quite detailed. Heavily academic
works, for detailed study of the Hebrew, are R.W. Klein's
1 Samuel (Word) and P.K. McCarter's *I Samuel* (Doubleday). S.R. Driver's *Notes on the Hebrew Text ... of ...
Samuel* (OUP), is still a guide to Hebrew grammatical points.
H.W. Hertzberg's *I and II Samuel* (SCM) is sometimes
destructive. C.F. Keil's *The Books of Samuel* (Eerdmans) is
still worth studying, although it is dated.

If you have enjoyed this book and would like to help us to send a copy of it and many other titles to needy pastors in the **Third World**, please write for further information or send your gift to:

Sovereign World Trust
PO Box 777, Tonbridge
Kent TN11 9XT
United Kingdom

or to the **'Sovereign World'** distributor in your country.

If sending money from outside the United Kingdom, please send an International Money Order or Foreign Bank Draft in STERLING, drawn on a **UK** bank to **Sovereign World Trust**.